73- 818 19

W9-DJF-188

The Catholic
Theological Union
LIBRARY
Chicago, Ill.

WITHDRAWN

ligion and Reason 8

hod and Theory
he Study and Interpretation of Religion

ERAL EDITOR
es Waardenburg, *University of Utrecht*

RD OF ADVISERS

. van Baaren, *Groningen*
Bellah, *Berkeley*
nz, *Marburg*
ianchi, *Bologna*
W. Drijvers, *Groningen*
Dupré, *Chicago*
Eisenstadt, *Jerusalem*
liade, *Chicago*
eertz, *Princeton*
oldammer, *Marburg*
icœur, *Paris*
Rodinson, *Paris*
mart, *Lancaster*
Widengren, *Uppsala*

OUTON · THE HAGUE · PARIS

2/12/74

Religion, Cu

Re

Met
in t

GEN
Jacqu

BOA
Th.P
R.N
E. B
U. F
H.J.
W.
S.N
M.
C. C
K. C
P. F
M.
N.
G.

M

Religion, Culture and Methodology

Papers of the Groningen Working-group
for the Study of Fundamental Problems
and Methods of Science of Religion

edited by
Th. P. van BAAREN and H. J. W. DRIJVERS
University of Groningen

The Catholic
Theological Union
LIBRARY
Chicago, Ill.

MOUTON · THE HAGUE · PARIS

This book was published with the aid of the Netherlands Organisation for the Advancement of Pure Research (Z.W.O)

Library of Congress Catalog Card Number: 73-81819
Jacket design by Jurriaan Schrofer
© 1973, Mouton & Co
Printed in the Netherlands by Mouton Printers

Preface

In 1968 the 'Groningen working-group for the study of fundamental problems and methods of science of religion' was founded. The group consisted then and still consists of mostly younger scholars, most of them sharing my own dissatisfaction with phenomenology of religion in the old style and eager to try new ways. We were agreed that this task needed a team of scholars.

In how far we have succeeded in our aims remains to be judged by the reader; we are conscious that we only offer a number of tentative results. Whatever the results, however, may turn out to be, we have enjoyed long evenings of animated and sometimes heated discussions but always in an atmosphere of mutual friendliness.

Part of the papers read in our meetings we present now, hoping to elicit a response that may stimulate our further discussions. We are a working-group, a number of individual scholars forming a team for specific purposes of research. There exists no Groningen school, at most a certain Groningen climate, although a few scholars from other Dutch universities have joined us. We form a group of equals, rather unstructured, more or less comparable to a band of African Pygmies; we do not conform to the model of a hierarchically structured group with a leader and his followers; we do not teach or preach a new scientific orthodoxy and we know no heretics.

The group consisted originally of the following members: Prof. Dr. Th. P. van Baaren, Prof. Dr. J. M. S. Baljon, Drs. H. Buning, Dr. H. J. W. Drijvers, Prof. Dr. H. G. Hubbeling, Drs. L. Leertouwer and Dr. H. te Velde. Baljon and Buning have left Groningen but new members participate in our discussion: Drs. L. P. van den Bosch, Drs. K. D. Jenner, Drs. A. C. Klugkist, Mgr. Dr. J. B. Möller, Drs. J. G. Oosten, Drs. A. J. Vink and Dr. J. D. J. Waardenburg.

From time to time scholars from various countries have done us the honour to join in our discussions. These hours have been fruitful and stimulating for our own work and I should like to thank them all for their kind interest in our undertaking.

Th. P. van Baaren

Contents

Preface, by Th. P. van Baaren   5

1. Theology, Philosophy and Science of Religion and their Logical
   and Empirical Presuppositions, by H. G. Hubbeling   9

2. Science of Religion as a Systematic Discipline: Some Introductory Remarks, by Th. P. van Baaren 35

3. Theory Formation in Science of Religion and the Study of the
   History of Religions, by H. J. W. Drijvers. 57

4. Inquiry into Religious Behaviour: A Theoretical Reconnais-
   sance, by L. Leertouwer 79

5. The Examination of Religious Concepts in Religious Anthropology, by J. G. Oosten   99

6. Research on Meaning in Religion, by J. D. J. Waardenburg . . 109

7. Religious Ethology: Some Methodological Remarks, by
   A. J. Vink 137

8. Epilogue, by H. J. W. Drijvers and L. Leertouwer 159

Index of Names 169

Theology, Philosophy and Science of Religion and their Logical and Empirical Presuppositions

1. INTRODUCTION

In this article we want to discuss the borderlines between theology, philosophy of religion, and science of religion. Further we want to throw some light on the respective logical and empirical presuppositions of these disciplines. We want especially to emphasize the relevance of the logical presuppositions, because these are very often overlooked. Many students of religion seem still to hold the dated opinion that there is only one kind of logic. Modern logic, however, has shown that there are many kinds of logic. In this article we will, of course, not give a complete account of all the problems of modern logic and their relevance to the study of religion today. We only want to give an outline of the varieties of logic in order to acquire a better insight into our problem: the relation of theology, philosophy of religion and science of religion. The varieties of logic find their counterpart in the varieties of philosophy of religion as we shall see. Further we want to face the question whether a study of religion in a neutral, objective and 'scientific' way is possible. Is it necessary for the student of religion to have some recourse to his own faith or at least to his own religious experience?

We will start with a certain preliminary, vague description of the disciplines mentioned above. We shall then try to make these descriptions more explicit. By *science of religion* we understand the study of phenomena that are denoted as religious, such as certain conceptions of god, certain cultic acts as prayer, the sacrificing of animals, etc., the beliefs in certain holy places, holy trees, stones, etc., the beliefs in a saviour, a life after death, etc. This study consists of as exact a description of these phenomena as possible, including an explanation of them, if such an explanation can be given. It also includes a study of religion as such. This study ought to be done in as neutral a way as possible, in that the student gives an objective and impartial description and explanation of the religious phenomena. Neither does he give a moral or other evaluation of these phenomena, nor does he inquire into the truth of them. He does not show his own religious or atheistic preferences and by no means does he try to defend them within the scope of his discipline, the science of religion. Of course, the student of religion has his own right to a personal religious or atheistic conviction and he has, of course, the right to defend it. But by doing so he transcends the limits of his discipline, the science of religion, and he enters into another discipline. Science of religion as such therefore is neutral, objective and impartial. Of course, there remain many problems here. We will come back to them later in this article.

Philosophy of religion can best be described as science of religion plus the study of the truth and value of the various religious statements. The impartiality of the student of religion mentioned above as a characteristic of science of religion has been taken away. The student of philosophy of religion may defend his own religious or atheistic position, provided he does so in a philosophical way. Therefore he is not allowed to refer to some doctrine of the church or some saying of a Holy Scripture as a final authority. He may only refer to rational arguments, including arguments from experience. We shall come to the various forms of philosophy of religion later in this article.

(Dogmatic) *theology* on the other hand is a discipline in which from the start the student is allowed to refer to an accepted authority such as the doctrine of the church or the Holy Scripture or some other authority. We shall see in this article that even then theology can be done in a 'scientific' way. Whether or not one will call theology a science is another question. It is not the purpose of this article to make a decision in this respect. We will only try to throw some light on various aspects of scientific method, leaving it to the reader where he will draw the exact borderline between scientific and non-scientific disciplines.

2. Model of Language-systems

In order to acquire a better insight into the structure of science we will give the following *model*, taking scientific activity as a kind of arranging language statements. This model is self-evident and instructive. It is not a kind of explanatory model that pretends to explain facts in nature or elsewhere. It is a kind of simplifying model, within which the explanatory theories can be developed. It is common practise in science to test certain theories in a simplified model, in which certain irrelevant aspects of the phenomena are not taken into consideration. If we have, for example, two experiments in physics and one is made one hour later than the other, we take for granted that the temperature is the same, although in an absolute sense this is not the case, but we take care that the difference is minimal and of no account. In the same way the following model is a simplification of scientific investigation, but what is left out is irrelevant to our purpose. The reader is, however, by no means obliged to accept this model. He may make another model. The only thing pretended here is that the relevant parts of another model can be translated into the following language model. A model is only used to acquire a better insight into the problems of scientific investigation. It also makes it easier for us to discuss the problems that arise. What is said later on in this article about the logical and empirical presuppositions is much more substantial to the argument of the article than the language model and is independent of it; it has its validity, whatever the use and validity of the language model may be. Nevertheless, in order to talk in a more concrete way about the problem of scientific investigation, we need some model and the following language model has its advantages, as we shall see.

We will now develop the model of language-systems as a means to talk more concretely about the problems that concern us. In every language-system we first have a vocabulary: these are the words of the system. Then we have rules (criteria) to make well formed formulae. These are the basic meaningful statements of our language-system. Next we need criteria (rules) to decide which statements are basically true and which are not. Let me illustrate this with an example. In arithmetic the vocabulary is formed by the numbers, among which we may distinguish between natural, rational, real numbers, etc. Further we need a set of operational signs such as '+', '−', '×', '=', etc. The set of numbers and the set of operational signs form the vocabulary of our arithmetical language-system. Now we need rules to decide which statements are basically meaningful and which are not. On the basis of these rules we can say that '$3+2=5$' is meaningful; so is '$10+11=101$'. The latter statement is false in our decimal arithmetical system, yet not meaningless. A statement like '$4++=-5$' would be meaningless in ordinary arithmetic. It is very important to distinguish meaningful and meaningless statements on the one hand and true and false statements on the other hand! After having established the criteria by which we can distinguish between meaningful and meaningless statements, we lay down criteria by which we can decide which statements are true and which are false. On the ground of these criteria we can determine that '$3+2=5$' is a true and '$10+11=101$' is a false statement in our decimal arithmetical system. How much all this is based on convention is proved by the fact that '$10+11=101$' is false in our decimal system, but not in the digital arithmetical system, where '$10+11=101$' is the equivalent of '$2+3=5$' in the decimal system.

Until now we have pointed out how to determine which are the basic meaningful and true statements in our language-system. These statements are thus the primitive or elementary statements of our language-system. In the scientific language-systems it is necessary to search for principles of arranging the primitive statements so that with the help of these principles we may acquire an optimal order of these primitive basic statements. These principles of arranging are usually called hypotheses. They cannot be found by convention, in contradistinction to the basic primitive statements. By optimal order mentioned above we understand the arranging of primitive statements with the help of a minimum number of principles of arrangement (i.e. a minimum number of hypotheses). These principles of arrangement must arrange a maximum number of primitive statements and the deduction of the primitive statements from the principles of arrangement must be as simple as possible (i.e. the strongest possible form of logic must be used; we come to this later). With the concept of 'optimal order' I have given in other words the principle of economy, a fundamental principle of all theory and science. This principle of economy thus consists of three constituents:

1. A minimum of principles of arrangement;
2. A deduction as simple as possible;
3. A maximal arrangement of primitive statements.

That the principle of economy is fundamental in science can be easily explained. It is for example more fundamental than the principle that a scientific theory must be able to produce predictions. We can show this in the following trivial way. Suppose we want to explain some phenomena in the world of stars. Suppose that now an astronomic theory A, consisting of a set of hypotheses p_1, p_2 ... p_n explains all these phenomena. We are, moreover, able to predict some unknown phenomena with the help of this set of hypotheses which are confirmed by later observations. Now should the power of prediction be the fundamental criterion of a scientific theory instead of the principle economy, then we could construct a competing theory B, consisting of the same set of hypotheses as theory A, to which, however, are added some unnecessary hypotheses p_{n+1} ... p_{n+m}, for example we could contrive the unnecessary hypothesis that somewhere in the galactic universe there are mountains made of green cheese. Now, the predictive power of theory B is not less than that of theory A. Theory B only produces some predictions that cannot be verified. But all the predictions of theory A are also predicted by theory B. Should the power of prediction be the fundamental criterion of a scientific theory we should not be able to decide between A and B. By the principle of economy we must decide for theory A. The power of prediction has shown itself to be a useful criterion in scientific theory, but it is a derived criterion, because it has shown itself to be helpful in acquiring an optimal order of arranging.

The structure of language-systems given so far is abstract enough to cover all scientific systems. In passing: in this article we take the words 'science' and 'scientific' in the same sense as the German words *Wissenschaft* and *wissenschaftlich* or the Dutch words *wetenschap* and *wetenschappelijk*, i.e. they refer also to the human and historical sciences. Therefore we speak also of science of religion (godsdienstwetenschap), although this may sound a little akward to the English mind, for in English the word 'science' is very often restricted to the natural sciences. The more extended use of the concept of 'science' is, however, also increasing in the English speaking world. We also speak of arranging the elementary statements in order to include as many scientific activities as possible. Arranging may consist in describing the elementary statements, but it also may consist in explaining them, etc.

If we take the principle of economy as the fundamental scientific criterion, we are able to defend that also disciplines like theology or philosophy may use at least a scientific method. In philosophical theology e.g. one can try to demonstrate that 'God' is necessary as a principle of arrangement to acquire an optimal order of all our data of reason and experience. Even dogmatic theology can fulfill the requirements of our language-systems. For example, one may consider the statements of the Bible as primitive statements and try to show that the principle of the Trinity is necessary for the arranging of these statements. The doctrine of the Trinity as such does not occur in the Bible, but one may try to defend it as an hypothesis. Opponents can try to show that the acceptance of the principle of the Trinity is unnecessary. There are of course many theological language-systems, differing from each other according to the primitive statements permitted in the system. The structural unity of all sciences and disciplines does not, of course, exclude many fundamental differences among them. We shall return to this question later in this article. We want first to face some questions with respect to our model of language-systems.

We pointed out above that the statement '$10 + 11 = 101$' was false in one arithmetical system and true in another. This is true for all statements with respect to the various language-systems. Further: what is meaningless in one system need not be so in another. In arithmetic a statement like '3 is red' is meaningless, but in a language-system consisting in classifying painting-colours in which every colour correlates with a certain number the statement '3 is red' makes good sense. The sentence 'God has created the world' is meaningless in the language-system of the natural sciences, but it is not so in (philosophical) theology. The statement 'water boils at 100 degrees (centigrade thermometer)' is meaningless in logic, but not in physics.

Further: what is a primitive statement in one system need not be so in another. The move in chess 'KP4' ('e2–e4' in Dutch notation) is elementary in the language-system of chess. But for the calligrapher who wants to put these signs into calligraphy, 'KP4' is no longer an elementary statement.

We stated above that the basic elementary statements are 'true by convention'. Many may object to this, arguing that in this way all truth becomes relativistic. This is not the case. The theory only says that *within a certain language system* the truth of certain elementary statements is no longer discussed. They are fixed by convention. But in another language-system these statements can be discussed and their truth can be critically examined. Let us give an example. The statement 'there lies a book' is a primitive (elementary) statement in the language-system of our daily life, but also in that of physics. The difficult philosophical problem of perception is not discussed in these language-systems. One might say that the physiological side of the problem of perception is discussed in physics. But this does not touch the philosophical side of the problem, because in physics too we already rely on our perceptions. Their truth is not discussed in physics. But in spite of the fact that the truth of perception is presupposed in many language-systems, its truth is challenged in others such as philosophy. The model of language-systems says that certain primitive statements are true by convention only because their truth is no longer challenged within a certain language-system. This does not mean that their truth was accepted arbitrarily. People may be 'forced' to accept certain primitive statements, such as 'there lies a book', because they are self-evident within a certain language-system.

3. Classification of Sciences according to their Method

We saw above that with the help of the model of language-systems a fundamental unity in the various disciplines can be shown in that they all observe the principle of economy; at least they all can do so. This unity of method does not exclude a great variety of variants. We will now shortly touch upon this problem and make some classification of the various disciplines according to their variety in method. The variants in method emerge according to the variety of the ways of acquiring and supplying the primitive statements, according to the variety of their ways of inference.

First we get a great division between those sciences that use exclusively a deductive method, such as logic, mathematics, etc., and the other sciences and theories that always use a combination of deduction and induction. Now it is very important for the structure of a science to know of what kind the elementary facts are and consequently the primitive statements that express these elementary facts. In some sciences these elementary facts can be extended *ad libitum*, at least in principle, by means of experiments. This is the case in the natural sciences. Here we find the so-called methodological circle of the empirical sciences in its purest form: observation (which produces the elementary statements (facts) of the language-system) — guess (i.e. to contrive hypotheses and theoretical concepts by means of inductive rules) — prediction (i.e. to predict from these hypotheses and theoretical concepts new facts using deductive rules) — check (i.e. to verify these predictions with the help of observations). Thus an optimal arrangement is obtained. There are, however, sciences, particularly human sciences such as psychology, sociology, etc., in which the objects, i.e. the people investigated, react to the investigation. Nobody starts a second test unchanged. Although therefore, in principle, there is no difference between natural sciences and human sciences, in that both use the same logical and empirical methods, the human sciences have their special problems, because the people investigated change under the investigation and react to it.

Then we have the great group of historical sciences to which also historical natural sciences such as astronomy (partly), geology, etc. belong. Here the given facts expressed by the primitive statements must be discovered and cannot be obtained *ad libitum* by making experiments. Therefore these facts cannot be increased according to our wishes (cf. also Frey, 1970). But here we can at least search for new sources of information with the help of historical and archaeological investigations. This is no longer the case in the following sciences. In these systems the rules and the criteria of other language-systems are studied (epistemology, foundations of sciences); or the given facts (and the parallel elementary statements) are found by the results of other sciences. These statements can also be arranged by the method of optimal arrangement sketched above. This is done for example in inductive metaphysics not based on a certain world-view. In this group of sciences too the scientific character is guaranteed by the scientific character of the given facts (statements) and the scientific method of the optimal arrangement. The case is different in those disciplines that still use the latter method, but do not obtain their elementary statements in a way that is free from any world-view. They gather their elementary statements with the help of a certain world-view and religious experience. This is the case in disciplines like world-view philosophy, theology, etc. It is very difficult to decide whether to call these disciplines scientific or not, for at least they *do* use a scientific method. Thus we get the following survey:

Theoretical disciplines (they all search for an optimal arrangement)

1. Deductive disciplines (logic; mathematics);
2. Inductive-deductive disciplines;
2.1. The given facts (elementary statements) can be increased *ad libitum* by experiments (natural sciences);
2.2. The objects react to the investigation (human sciences);
2.3. The given facts (elementary statements) cannot be increased *ad libitum*, but they can be searched for in a direct, scientific way (historical sciences);
2.4. The given facts (elementary statements) can only be increased indirectly, because the discipline is built upon other disciplines (scientific inductive metaphysics) or studies the criteria and foundations of the other disciplines (epistemology, foundations of sciences);
2.5. The given facts (elementary statements) are obtained with the help of world-view and religious experience (world-view philosophy; theology).

Now returning to our topic, the relation of science of religion, philosophy of religion and theology, we may state that theology clearly belongs to the group of disciplines mentioned above sub 2.5. Philosophy of religion is a more complicated matter; we will discuss this more extensively below. Some philosophies of religion clearly belong to the group mentioned sub 2.5.; some to the group mentioned sub 2.4.

Science of religion on the other hand partly belongs to the group mentioned sub 2.2., partly to the group mentioned sub 2.3. Its elementary statements are traced by means of ordinary historical methods, such as the investigation of religious documents, old descriptions, etc. But also modern methods of social sciences are applied, especially but not exclusively in the study of the living religions. In the Groningen discussion group on methodology of science of religion (*methodiek van de gods-*

dienstwetenschap), for which this paper was primarily produced, religion is studied as a form of culture. Now it is not denied that some questions may be raised here, but whatever the difficulties in this science may be, it is not necessary to refer to the world-view of the investigator as a source of knowledge or a criterion of truth. We will return to this question below.

4. Varieties of Experience

In all the disciplines, with the exception of logic and mathematics, there are two sources of knowledge: logic and experience. The logical source of knowledge will be our next point of discussion in the following pages; we will first give some attention to the other source of knowledge. We have already referred to it indirectly in our discussion above. It is a non-formal source of knowledge that provides us with the elementary statements in the various language-systems. We want to take 'experience' here in a broad sense. It is that which gives us information about the outer world. By it I know that there is a book on the table, that it is raining outside, etc. We will call this kind of experience 'ordinary experience' in contradistinction to, for example, ethical and religious experience. The latter two are, by the way, kinds of experience too. Now even 'ordinary experience' provides us with many philosophical problems. If we see a book on the table, we cannot pretend that we come to this conclusion by the help of sense experience alone. But it would transcend the limits of this article, to go into all these philosophical problems. For our purpose it is sufficient to consider the language-systems, in which sentences such as 'I see a book on the table' or even 'there is a book on the table' are taken to be elementary. In ordinary life the truth of such sentences is not in doubt. For science of religion the basic elementary sentences are of this sort. They are provided by religious documents, by reports of religious experience and they are as such not called into question. Now in the disciplines mentioned above sub 2.1., 2.2. and 2.3. the empirical source of knowledge consists in this 'ordinary experience', moulded of course by the various scientific methods. The many problems in philosophy of science which can be raised here, we will leave aside.

The only thing we want to point out is that science of religion does not transcend this 'ordinary experience'. On some questions that may arise here, we will touch later. Of course, science of religion deals with statements of religious experience of other people. The investigator deals with them carefully and with an open mind. But in this science he should not base judgments on religious experiences of his own. As to philosophy of religion the matter is much more complicated. There are many possibilities here. In the first place many logical systems are possible here. We come to these next. But also with respect to experience there are several possibilities. One can build up one's philosophy of religion on 'ordinary experience', but one can also build a 'stronger' system in which the investigator may refer to his own religious experience. And even with respect to this religious experience a distinction is possible. One can for example refer to mystical experience only, without accepting the other forms of religious experience. By mystical experience in this connection we would understand those experiences that are obtained by means of special contemplative and 'prayer' techniques that are common in many religions. We think especially of the various stages that finally lead to a *unio mystica* (Heiler, 1923: 312 ff.). Now such experience may be distinguished from those religious experiences which lead one, for example, to accept a set of church doctrines as true. In the way we use the word 'religious experience' it might be clear that we use it in a broad sense. It also includes a possible religious intuition. It is not necessary that he who uses this term, should go through a state of great emotional exaltation. The only thing emphasized here is, that people who refer to it, mean by it something different from logic or, 'ordinary experience' and refer to it as a source that gives religious knowledge. And religious knowledge includes in this connection knowledge about God or gods, his plan with the world, his saving actions, etc.

5. Varieties of Logic

We will now deal with the various logical systems that are relevant to our problem. We would call the reader's attention especially to this part of the article, for there are many misunderstandings here. Until the rise of modern logic since the end of the last century, it was an accepted truth that there was only one form of logic and even now many stick to this misunderstanding. On the other hand the various (non–dialectical) logical systems (we explain the term 'dialectical' below) are no competing systems in the sense that in one logical system a theorem is proved to be true that is proved to be false in another system. The situation is this, that in some systems theorems are proved to be true that cannot be proved in other logical systems. By logic we want to understand the science (or art) of correct reasoning. Logic teaches us how to infer a conclusion from a set of premises. Now some logical systems permit us to draw a conclusion which others do not. The logical systems in which less conclusions can be drawn are called more strict; the systems in which more conclusions can be drawn are called stronger. In this article we want to avoid the word 'weaker' that is sometimes used in an ambiguous way as a contradistinction to both! The use of the words 'more strict' and 'stronger' are in our opinion self-evident. Of course, it cannot be the purpose of this article to give an exposé of all the logical systems and their merits. We must restrict ourselves to a short summary of what is relevant to our article.

The most strict logical system of all the systems that are usual is *intuitionistic* or *constructivistic* logic. This means that in this system the drawing of conclusions is submitted to very strict rules and that several conclusions are not permitted to be drawn. This system is mainly characterized by the fact that the theorem of excluded middle is not valid. This means that the following theorem is not valid in this system:

(1)   '$p \vee -p$' (here '$\vee$' = the sign for disjunction; it is translated in ordinary language by 'or'; '$-$' is the sign for negation; '$-p$' means 'not p'; and 'p' represents a proposition).

In (1) we have expressed the theorem of excluded middle in a logical artificial language. It might be translated in ordinary language in the following way: 'Either a proposition itself or its negation is true'. This theorem is not valid in intuitionistic logic. The following theorem is connected with (1) and is therefore not valid either in intuitionistic logic:

(2)   'p is equivalent to $-(-p)$'

In (2) it is stated that a proposition is equivalent to the negation of its negation. This has its consequences in proof theory. In mathematics and in other sciences very often the proof method of *reductio ad absurdum* is used. Now this method has only a restricted validity in intuitionistic logic. The following way of inference is valid: 'Suppose *p*. From *p* we infer a contradiction. Therefore: —*p*, i.e. the negation of *p* is true'. But the following way of reasoning is not valid: 'Suppose —*p*. From —*p* we infer a contradiction. Therefore: *p*, i.e. we conclude from the contradiction to which the negation of *p* leads to the truth of *p*'. This kind of reasoning is not valid in intuitionistic logic. From the contradiction to which —*p* leads we may only infer to —(—*p*), which is not equivalent to *p* in intuitionistic logic as we have seen. Although intuitionistic logic has its merits in that it is very strict, it is on the whole too strict to be practical. Many important parts of mathematics can no longer be proved and among these are many parts that are of high practical relevance (Kleene, 1967: 46 ff.).

The standard system in philosophy and science is *classical logic*. Classical logic in this sense includes modern symbolic logic. If one wants to make a distinction between modern logic and for example Aristotelian or scholastic logic, the latter two are denoted by *traditional logic*. Classical logic is used in contradistinction to the intuitionistic logic mentioned above. In this logic. the theorems mentioned sub (1) and (2) are valid. also in proof theory the *reductio ad absurdum* is also valid in the second form mentioned above. Classical logic is used regularly in the sciences; it is not a suspect system such as dialectical logic, a kind of logic we mean to discuss in due time. But before doing so we shall first refer to some extensions in logic that have both their intuitionistic and classical variants.

In the first place there is the so called *modal logic*. This is the logic of the words 'possible', 'contingent', 'necessary', etc. A *deontic logic* is also known: a logic concerning the words 'obligated', 'permissible', etc. Then there is a *logic of probablity*, a *logic of knowing and belief*, etc. In principle there is no limit to these extensions. They permit us to translate every sentence in a natural language into its equivalent in a logical artificial language. In this way it is possible to check all reasonings. This translation, by the way, has only this purpose. It is of course not possible to translate all the emotional overtones and associations that go with the sentences in the natural languages. Only in so far as conclusions are drawn in natural languages, they can be checked by translation into an artificial logical language.

The extensions mentioned above are modifications of propositional logic. The various propositions are modified by words like 'possible', etc. Within a proposition the *logic of predicates* and the *logic of relations* help us in the translation. All these systems have their intuitionistic and classical variants. In most sciences one has no need to resort to any logical system that is less strict (and stronger) than classical logic with its variants in modal logic, logic of probability, etc. In various philosophical systems, however, many stronger logical systems are uncritically used, because their inference rules have a certain plausibility. We shall show, however, that they cannot be universally valid.

The systems that are less strict and therefore stronger than the systems of classical logic are very often called systems of *dialectical logic*. Here too, many variations are possible. First we shall discuss a system that we want to call the *dialectical logic of the infinite* or the *dialectical logic of the absolute*. The rule of inference that is used in this system has a certain intuitive plausibility and during many centuries it was used in philosophy without any doubt as to its validity. Even now, we are tempted to use it, if we are not on our guard.

Speaking informally, in this system of dialectics of the infinite an inference is permitted from the finite to the infinite, or from the relative to the absolute. This rule of inference from the finite to the infinite or from the relative to the absolute has a certain tempting plausibility and it is quite understandable that during many centuries this rule was practised without any doubts. The reasoning goes for example as follows: 'There are degrees of certainty; then we must postulate a degree of absolute certainty in order to measure the various degrees of certainty'. Or: 'there are many different forms of loyalty. There is a relation of a human I to a human thou. Now the loyalty of human relations is only relative. Therefore there must be a source of absolute loyalty from which the relative human forms of loyalty derive their strength'. A classical example of this way of reasoning we find in the fourth way of Thomas Aquinas: 'The fourth way is based on the gradation observed in things. Some things are found to be more good, more true, more noble, and so on, and other things less. But such comparative terms describe varying degrees of approximation to a superlative; for example, things are hotter and hotter the nearer they approach what is hottest. Something therefore is the truest and best and most noble of things, and hence the most fully in being; ... There is something therefore which causes in all things their being, their goodness, and whatever other perfection they have. And this we call 'God' (Thomas Aquinas, 1967, 15 ff.).

This is a clear example of the rule of inference mentioned above. We will not deny that it has a certain plausibility. Still it is not universally valid. The Amsterdam professor of logic and philosophy of science E. W. Beth has formalized this rule and in doing so he has clearly shown its limits (Beth, 1946: 260, 1952: 66-68). We will give his formalization in a slightly simplified way.

Let there be given a set of elements: a_1, a_2, a_3, etc. and let also an ordering relation R be given. This means that a_1 stands in the relation R to a_2, a_2 stands in the relation R to a_3, etc. In symbolic notation: $a_1 R a_2$, $a_2 R a_3$, etc. We will skip over the various technical aspects of set theory here, for they are of no relevance to our purpose. Now according to the rule of inference in the dialectics of infinity there must be a last element.

With respect to this last element the following is valid: there is no longer any element to which this last element stands in the relation R, except possibly to itself; and all the other elements stand in the relation R to this last element. In other words: let us call this last element a_n, then the following two theorems are valid

(3) $a_x R a_n$

(4) $-(a_n R a_x)$

where a_x stands for any arbitrary element in the ordered set of elements different from a_n and '$-$' is the usual sign for negation.

Let us give some concrete examples: Let a_1, a_2, a_3, etc. be various periods of time with their various social systems and let R mean 'is succeeded by'; then in orthodox Marxism the following conclusion is valid: there finally must be a communist period which will be the last period in history. Any period succeeding it, would still be the period of communism and this period will make an end to all class struggle, etc. In other words a_n is the period of communism.

Another example: let a_1, a_2, a_3, etc. be the facts in this world and let R be the relation 'being caused by', then a_n is God. Here we have formalized the second way of Thomas Aquinas.

Thanks to Beth's formalization, however, we can show in a rather trivial way that this rule of dialects of infinity is not universally valid. Let for example a_1, a_2, a_3, etc. be the row of natural numbers (starting with number 1) and let R be the ordering relation: 'smaller than'; then we get the following sequence: '1 smaller than 2', '2 smaller than 3', etc. Should the rule of dialectics of infinity be valid, then we would be permitted to conclude that there must be a number a_n, of which it could be said that no number a_{n+1} can be found, of which can be stated '$a_n R a_{n+1}$'. In other words there could be found a greatest possible number. Now it is clear that this is not true.

On the other hand it is clear that the rule is sometimes valid. Let for example R be the relation 'greater than' and let a_1, a_2, a_3 be natural numbers again, a_1 being 100, then we may get a sequence like '100 greater than 99', '99 greater than 98', etc. Is there now a number a_n for which no number a_{n+1} can be found, of which can be said '$a_n R a_{n+1}$'? This is certainly true. If we do not count the number 0 to the natural numbers, the number 1 is a_n.

Furthermore in classical set theory (not in intuitionistic set theory!) a certain theorem, Zorn's lemma, is known, in which the rule of inference of the dialectics of infinity is valid, provided that special conditions are fulfilled: 'Let A be a non-empty partially ordered set in which every totally ordered subset has an upper bound in A. Then A contains at least one maximal element' (Lipschutz, 1964: 180). We mention Zorn's lemma here only for the sake of curiosity. It would take us too far to explain this lemma and to point out its philosophical implications. But it might be clear that it means that the inference rule of dialectics of infinity may be drawn, provided one has proved that the conditions of Zorn's lemma are fulfilled. Besides the dialectics of infinity we also have *Hegelian dialectics*. It would take us too far should we go into all the facets of this dialectics. Lenin has summarized 16 aspects of it (Lenin, 1960: 212-214). We give the following points. It might be possible that certain thinkers accept only a part of them as valid. Hegelian dialectics is characterized by (i) the development by means of contradictions; (ii) the negation of the negation (after thesis, antithesis, a synthesis will follow that is not a repetition of the thesis; see for the differences with classical logic theorem (2) mentioned above). This negation of the negation was omitted by Joseph Stalin; it was restored by his successors, in conformity with the theories of Lenin, Engels, Marx and Hegel; (iii) the thought that the concrete elements in reality can never be fully subsumed under a general rule. A concrete element always adds something new to the abstract general rule. Thus in the synthesis concrete (in contradistinction to abstract) generality is reached. Parallel thoughts we can find in the hermeneutical method of Gadamer; (iv) all finite individual elements are to be interpreted by the (infinite) whole. Thus Hegelian dialectics presupposes the dialectics of infinity and adds new inference rules to it. It is not the place here to discuss the merits of Hegelian dialectics. It is even more suspect than the dialectics of infinity, in that it is so vague and ambiguous that it is not even capable of being formalized. Although the author of this article does not commit himself to this kind of dialectics, he acknowledges that classical logic still has its deficiencies too especially in the constructing of the conceptual system for explaining time processes. It might be that Hegelian dialectics can give a substantial contribution here. The present author, however, has more confidence in the continual building up of more extensive logical systems based on classical logic. But this task, he admits, is by no means fulfilled yet. A *chronological logic* has been developed but the time concept that is basic here, is what is sometimes called mechanical time. It is the time concept that is basic for a so-called Markov process, i.e. a process in which each following phase is completely determined by its immediate predecessor, while all other phases preceding them are irrelevant. Now historical processes are not of that kind. The more remote past is always exerting its influence on later times. But we should be able to construct a logic for these historical processes too.

6. FINAL CHARACTERIZATION OF SCIENCE OF RELATION

According to our opinion science of religion has no need to resort to logical systems stronger (and less strict) than classical logic. Hegelian dialectics leads to too subjective an application to be called fruitful for science. As a partly historical science, science of religion cannot profit very much from the development of modern logic, as other sciences do nowadays (mathematics, linguistics, etc.). But even in science of religion modern logic can give a more substantial contribution than it usually does. It would transcend the limits of this article, should we go into a more detailed discussion of it here. We will only refer to the following point. This is not only relevant to science of religion, but to every historical science. In many historical arguments we meet the word 'probable' and even if we do not meet it, it is indirectly presupposed. Now in mathematics and physics also many processes are only probable, but here we can very often give the exact probability of their truth or outcome. Because this is not possible in historical processes we are tempted to use this notion without much critical reflection. Modern logic is, however, able to give a conceptual apparatus that includes the vagueness of the probability of historical processes, while still maintaining a degree of exactness which makes it a desirable instrument. Thus we may avoid plausible mistakes. Let us give an example, avoiding all technical details. Suppose that we give an historical argument that is built upon a chain of arguments, each of which has a great degree of probability. Now we are not able to give the exact degree of this probability. So a theory of probability in history is needed. There are of course cases in history where the probability of their being true is so great that the probability of their negation can be neglected. But very often arguments are used the negation of which has at least some degree of probability. We should realize that if we have a chain of arguments of this last kind of probability, our conclusion has a degree of probability that is much less. Let us suppose that we could agree in historical sciences to give arguments that are not beyond doubt a degree of probability not higher than 0.9, if our scale of probability is from 0 to 1. We should realize that a chain of, for example, four of such arguments gives us a probability for the conclusion of at most $0.9 \times 0.9 \times 0.9 \times 0.9 = 0.6561$, which is not to be called probable at all. Using such arguments carelessly we do not realize that our conclusion has become no longer probable, because to our 'feeling' the arguments themselves have a great degree of probability, so that we are tempted to suppose that our conclusion has the same degree of probability. Also other examples of the relevance of the logic or calculus of probability for historical sciences can be given. Sometimes we come to a conclusion not by a chain of arguments, but by giving an addition of arguments.

If these arguments are independent of each other, then, taken together, they may make the conclusion highly probable, even if they themselves have not such a high degree of probability. Two independent arguments with a degree of probability of 0.6 yield already a conclusion of 0.84 $(0.6 + 0.6 - 0.6 \times 0.6)$.

We have until now defended a rather 'scientific' approach in science of religion (and we will do the same for philosophy of religion, as we shall see). Now many objections might be raised here. We will discuss the most important of them, restricting ourselves in this article to two main counterarguments.

In the first place, very often the impartial, objective approach defended above, is argued to be impossible in historical science, because in history the preferences of the historical investigator cannot be left out. He might consider himself to be as impartial as possible, he will always show his own preferences in the selection of his material, in the way he puts the problems, etc. and in doing so he is subjective and not impartial. We will not deny that the personal preferences of the investigator cannot always be avoided. But this does not permit the investigator to be simply partial in his approach. Let us consider more carefully in what his 'subjectivism' consists. Of course, out of the vast material of basic elementary sentences of the language-system of his investigation the investigator will choose those which he thinks most important for his investigation. And, of course, his personal preferences may guide his selection. But these basic sentences as such are not subjective and their truth can be checked by anybody. Should his selection of the basic sentences be incomplete in some relevant aspects, then his fellow investigators can correct him in the same way as in other sciences. If we use the scientific method as sketched above, all his theories are corrigible. It may take some time before a tempting theory is refuted, but in principle it is always possible. His possible subjective preference can be countered by other investigators.

Another related objection is the following. Some investigators of the more hermeneutical schools defend the thesis that what is really relevant to the investigation is the personal capacity of the investigator to 're-experience' the religious feelings and conceptions expressed in the material he is studying. And in contradistinction to this we have denied above the necessity for the investigator to have religious experiences himself. Now we shall not deny that a certain kind of sympathy and interest in the object studied is fruitful for every investigation. This is true for every historical and other investigation. But these are the psychological presuppositions of the investigation that have nothing to do with the methodology of the investigation as such. Every theory (set of hypotheses) should be checked by the basic sentences (facts) of our study and not by some sympathetic inner feeling or personal re-experience.

In our opinion such a method is the only way to make real progress in science of religion and to penetrate deeper into it. And although we have pointed out above that there are differences between the natural, human and historical sciences, they all have a dominating structure in common. As H. Albert has pointed out (1970: 3 ff.), there is no need to base historical sciences on a reconstruction of 'inner experiences' of individuals by means of a sympathetic method of understanding (*verstehende Methode*). The latter is, as a specific historical method, very often opposed to the method of searching for general laws in natural sciences (Droysen, 1960: 330 ff.). This opposition is considered obsolete by most methodologists. We agree, however, with those methodologists who defend the relative relevance of the hermeneutical method to the *inventing* of new hypotheses. The same is true for world-view metaphysics (Albert, 1970; Stegmüller, 1969; Wartofsky, 1967; De Groot, 1969). They may inspire investigators to a new view on old problems. The same holds for incorrect theories. There are fruitful mistakes in science! As complete systems e.g. Marx' and Freud's theories are incorrect, but they have opened our eyes to powers in human life that had until then been undiscovered. Furthermore, I admit that the great scientific discoveries do not always follow from pure scientific presuppositions (Kuhn, 1970). They are not made in a continuous chain without interruption. But that has to do with the inventing of hypotheses and not with the building up of scientific systems as such (cp. also Kiesel, 1971). Moreover, Kuhn rightly points out that the conceptual scheme of a science reflects the spiritual climate of its time to a certain extent. It is very important to realize that a change in a conceptual scheme produces a different theory. All these admissions, however, do not change our methodological view-point. For they are already presupposed in our exposition. Changes in conceptual schemes primarily produce different basic sentences (base facts). And thus one gets different theories. If, however, different theories proceed from different basic sentences, we are not concerned with competing theories, but with theories that are complementary to each other. We may compare such a situation with the two theories of light in physics. The wave theory and the corpuscular theory are not, strictly speaking, competing theories. The basic facts explained by the two theories differ according to the various experiments (Beth, 1953: 112ff.). In the same way fruitful conceptual schemes are complementary to each other. Theories based on such schemes are always open to public or intersubjective testing, a possibility that is ruled out, if one resorts to one's 'inner experiences'. Another objection against our methodological position may be raised on the grounds that the axiomatic and deductive part in our theory of language-systems is dominant. But, as Bunge has pointed out (1970: 204) '... axiomatics is scientifically valuable because it renders explicit all the assumptions actually employed and so makes it possible to keep them under control'. Moreover, modern logical insight has definitely shown that all inductive procedures are based upon deductive ones (Bochenski, 1954: 100ff.; V. Kraft, 1970). Our methodological position has, in our opinion, the advantage of incorporating the merits of the logical positivistic methodologies without taking over their positivistic metaphysics.

So from our methodological considerations the following conclusion may be drawn. In science of religion we should be as strict as possible. Therefore we should restrict ourselves to classical logic and 'ordinary experience' and until now there are no reasons to resort to stronger systems, stronger in logic or stronger in experience. Here, as the reader may notice, we have extended the use of the words 'stronger' and 'strict' also to the experiential side of our knowledge. A system based on, for example, 'ordinary experience' and religious experience might be called stronger than a system based on 'ordinary experience' alone. And also here the rule is valid, that our treatment should be as simple as possible, that is we should suppose as little as possible. Until now we need directly or indirectly classical logic; as far as we can see we cannot confine ourselves to intuitionistic logic. But even here the rule is valid, that if we can give a positive proof of the truth of a certain proposition 'p', this is better than only refuting its negation.

7. VARIETIES OF PHILOSOPHY OF RELIGION

In philosophy of religion many systems are possible. The most strict system confines itself to classical logic and 'ordinary experience'. One should not immediately reproach such a philosophy of religion with the argument that its results are too meagre. We admit that, but it is still interesting to see how far one can get in such a strict system. It is even possible to prove God's existence in such a system. Or better, we can prove in such a system the existence of an *ens necessarium* with the help of the modal logical system S_5, that is the classical variant in the sequence of modal systems, S_4 being more or less the equivalent of the intuitionistic system. It is customary in modal logic to indicate the strictness of the modal systems by an indexnumber placed below the letter S. The stricter the system, the lower its indexnumber. As the reader sees the systems S_1 to S_3 are even more strict than S_4, the intuitionistic system. S_5 is a formalization of the 'classical' system in use since the day of Theophrastus (Hughes and Cresswell, 1968). The proof of the existence of an *ens necessarium* can be given in the system S_5, not in S_4 (Hubbeling, 1971: 91 ff. §8.15 ff.). The usual interpretation of 'necessary' in this connection is 'what occurs in all possible conceivable worlds', or 'what is true in all possible conceivable worlds'. This *ens necessarium* can be given some content. It can be proved that it is 'good' in the sense that it is the ground of all being, that it has an ego-structure in that it is self reflexive, etc. It would, however, transcend the limits of this article should we go into details here. But we immediately admit that the proof of a Christian God or the truth of some theses of the Christian faith cannot be given in such a strict system. If one wants to go further and to give a more fully developed philosophy of religion, then various ways are open. The investigator can make the logical part of his system stronger and apply the dialectics of infinity or Hegelian dialectics. As the latter include the dialectics of infinity and even add some rules of inference to it, it is stronger (and less strict) than the dialectics of infinity. The present author would resist an application of Hegelian dialectics. This system is too vague and ambiguous. Moreover, as the law of non-contradiction is not valid here, both 'p' and '$-p$' may be deducible in such a system and that means that in principle anything can be deduced in the system. Now a system in which anything can be deduced is worthless from a scientific point of view. The present author would also resist a naive application of the dialectics of infinity. Personally he would prefer to refrain totally from it in the present stage of investigation, but we saw that in principle the inference rules in the system can be reformulated so as to make them acceptable from a scientific point of view. In our opinion a recourse to mystical and religious experience is more fruitful than the help of doubtful logical systems. It would, however, again be beyond the scope of this article to give an account of all these possibilities. Still the reader may see the relevance of indicating exactly what kind of system of philosophy of religion the investigator is using. Very often the presupposed logic and experience are not clearly indicated. Moreover, opponents are very often measured by a much stricter standard than one's own system! An example of this fallacy may be found in the work of W. Pannenberg (1967). Pannenberg criticizes the proofs of God's existence in the traditional way, thus using classical logic. In his own exposé he uses a kind of Hegelian logic, in which all the refuted proofs of God's existence could be proved again! (cf. Hubbeling, 1970).

It should be clear that this is not acceptable. Philosophers of religion should avoid this and clearly indicate what kind of system they are using. Then at least many misunderstandings would disappear and the discussion would be held in a more scientific way.

Also in theology the doubtful logical systems can and should be avoided. A clear commitment to obedience to (a part of) Holy Scripture or any other authority is, from a scientific point of view, clearer than the indirect and unspoken introduction of doubtful systems and the using of ambiguous rules of inference.

REFERENCES

Albert, H. (1970) 'Theorie, Verstehen und Geschichte. Zur Kritik des methodologischen Autonomieanspruchs in den sogenannten Geisteswissenschaften', *Zeitschrift für allgemeine Wissenschaftstheorie/Journal for General Philosophy of Science*, I, 1 (1970), pp. 3-23.

Beth, E.W. (1953), *Inleiding tot de wijsbegeerte der exacte wetenschappen*. Antwerpen/Amsterdam, Standaard-Boekhandel.

— (1946), 'Historical Studies in Traditional Philosophy', *Synthese*, 5 (1946-1947), pp. 258-270.

— (1952), 'The Prehistory of Research into Foundations', *The British Journal for the Philosophy of Science*, 3 (1952-1953), pp. 58-81.

Bochenski, I.M. (1954), *Die zeitgenössischen Denkmethoden*. Bern, A. Francke Verlag.

Bunge, M. (1970) 'The Physicist and Philosophy', *Zeitschrift für allgemeine Wissenschaftstheorie/Journal for General Philosophy of Science*, I, 2 (1970), pp. 196-209.

De Groot, A.D. (1969), *Methodology; Foundations of Inference and Research in the Behavioral Sciences*. The Hague, Mouton.

Droysen, J.G. (1960), *Historische Vorlesungen über Enzyklopädie und Methodologie der Geschichte*. München, R. Oldenbourg.

Frey, G. (1970), 'Hermeneutische und hypothetisch-deduktive Methode', *Zeitschrift für allgemeine Wissenschaftstheorie/Journal for General Philosophy of Science*, I, 1 (1970), pp. 24-41.

Heiler, F. (1923), *Das Gebet. Eine religionsgeschichtliche und religionspsychologische Untersuchung*, 5. Auflage. München, Ernst Reinhardt.

Hubbeling, H.G. (1970), 'Einige kritische Fragen an Pannenberg', *Kerk en Theologie*, 21, 4 (oktober 1970), pp. 246-359.

— (1971), *Language, Logic and Criterion. A Defence of Non-Positivistic Logical Empiricism*. Amsterdam Assen, Born.

Hughes, G.E., and Cresswell, M.J. (1968), *An Introduction to Modal Logic*. London, Methuen.

Kiesel, Th. (1971), 'Zu einer Hermeneutik naturwissenschaftlicher Entdeckung', *Zeitschrift für allgemeine Wissenschaftstheorie/Journal for General Philosophy of Science*, II, 2 (1971), pp. 195-222.

Kleene, S.C. (1967), *Introduction to Metamathematics*. Amsterdam, North-Holland Publishing Co./Groningen, P. Noordhoff.

Kuhn, Th.S. (1970), The 'Structure of Scientific Revolutions', in O. Neurath, R. Carnap and Ch. Morris (ed.), *Foundations of the Unity of Science. Toward* an *International Encyclopedia of Unified Science*, Vol. II, pp. 53-273. Chicago, The University of Chicago Press.

Lenin, W.I. (1960), *Werke*, Band 38 (*Philosophische Hefte*). Berlin, Dietz Verlag.

Lipschutz, S. (1964), *Set Theory and Related Topics*. New York, Schaum Publishing Co.

Pannenberg, W. (1967), *Grundfragen systematischer Theologie. Gesammelte Aufsätze*. Göttingen, VandenHoeck und Ruprecht.

Stegmüller, W. (1969), *Probleme und Resultate der Wissenschaftstheorie und Analytische Philosophie, Band I, Wissenschaftliche Erklärung und Begründung*. Berlin, Springer Verlag.

Thomas Aquinas (1964), *Summa Theologiae. Latin Text and English Translation*, Vol. 2. London, Dyre and Spottiswoode.

Wartofsky, M.W. (1967), 'Metaphysics as Heuristic for Science', in R. Cohen and M.W. Wartofsky (ed.), *Boston Studies in the Philosophy of Science*, Vol. III (*In Memory of Norwood Russell Hanson*). Dordrecht, D. Reidel.

Science of Religion as a Systematic Discipline
Some Introductory Remarks

There are a great many definitions of religion, but a generally accepted one is still lacking. E. Norbeck begins 'merely defining religion is obviously not difficult' but he finishes by saying 'a definition which might satisfy all ... is ... impossible and undesirable to realize' (Norbeck, 1961: 3). The first remark may be true but I cannot agree that it is undesirable to search for a definition of religion, even if it is not generally accepted. U. Bianchi rightly states: 'Die religionsgeschichtliche Forschung sieht sich zunächst einem vorwegzunehmenden Problem gegenüber, ... Umfang und Inhalt des Begriffes Religion. Es handelt sich also darum zu bestimmen auf welche Phänomene die religionsgeschichtliche Forschung sich zu erstrecken hat, welche Phänomene sich noch als religiös bezeichnen lassen, wenn auch nur hinsichtlich einer niedrigen, rudimentären oder in Verfall begriffenen Religiösität, und welche dagegen auf andersgeartete geistige Standpunkte zurückzuführen sind' (Bianchi, 1964: 5).

I restrict myself to quoting a few recent definitions. A. Leroi-Gourhan gives a very short definition of religion which has to serve for the interpretation of prehistoric material: 'Les manifestations des préoccupations paraissant dépasser l'ordre matériel' (Leroi-Gourhan, 1964: 5). This concise definition can be useful on many occasions but it has the drawback that no clear distinction is made between art and religion.

C. Geertz tries to give a wholly sociological definition, especially adapted to the study of ritual. According to him religion is '(1) a system of symbols which acts to (2) establish powerful, pervasive, and long-lasting moods and motivations in men by (3) formulating conceptions of a general order of existence and (4) clothing these conceptions with such an aura of factuality that (5) the moods and motivations seem uniquely realistic' (Geertz, 1966: 4). This definition has the advantage that all theological or metaphysical presuppositions have been eliminated; it is, however, one-sided because the beings and powers in whose existence the religions believe are totally ignored.

This objection is shared by M.R. Spiro who protests against a definition of religion which chooses to ignore the belief in 'superhuman' beings. He defines religion as 'an institution consisting of culturally patterned interaction with culturally postulated superhuman beings' (Spiro, 1966: 96). This definition accentuates three important points: the institutional character of religion, the interaction between mankind and gods, etc., and the belief on which this interaction is stated to be founded by the believers. The objection to this definition is that it is insufficiently detailed.

In a controversial but interesting book G. Swanson rightly points out that 'magic and religion remain distinctive in having contacts with the supernatural as their goal' (Swanson, 1968: 10).

To avoid the pretention of being able to give a better definition of religion, I shall limit myself to an effort at circumscription, by giving a general description of what I mean when I use the term religion. In this effort I will make intensive and extensive use of the definitions given by Geertz and Spiro, but without following their terminology in all respects, while I shall give some additions which I think necessary.

1. Religion is a function of culture and is connected with and interacts with other functions of culture.

There are many definitions of culture; I only quote two, which in different words mainly state the same thing. B. Malinowski says that culture is 'a vast apparatus, partly material, partly human and partly spiritual, by which man is able to cope with the concrete specific problems that face him' (Malinowski, 1960: 63). R. Piddington defines culture as 'the sum total of the material and intellectual equipment whereby they (sc. men) satisfy their biological and social needs and adapt themselves to their environment' (Piddington, 1952: 3). In short, culture is all that is learned.

It is, of course, self-evident that religions may be influenced by other cultures, or functions of other cultures and in their turn may exert such an influence.

From our statement that religion is a function of culture, it follows that religion should be studied in connection with other functions of culture such as social order, art, economics, law, etc.

The term function is used in its general sense as a way or form of expression, e.g. bodily functions, and does not imply that the approach advocated is that of functionalism in the full sense of the word.

The first remark is not meant to deny religion its own specific character within the framework of a culture, neither would I neglect the fact that most religions claim a supercultural cause for their existence. However, giving attention to what a religion proclaims about its own existence, does not mean that science of religion has to accept these statements without criticism as the ultimate source of our knowledge for the religion in question. Science of religion has no reason to accord higher value to what a religion states about itself than to a report by others, because it is not at all sure that in all cases self-understanding is essentially better than the understanding others may have.

It may even be doubted whether the adherents of a certain ideological or belief system are as a rule capable of surveying and seeing through the roots, connections and consequences of their own system, unless they have been educated to do this by a special scientific training. As has been said before 'no social phenomenon can be adequately studied merely in the language and categories of thought in which the people among whom it is found represent it to themselves' (Hardt, 1966: 123). This means that every discipline needs a meta-language.

According to structuralism the structure of a given system is not conscious. One also learns one's own language without needing to become conscious of the underlying structure. G. Schiwy writing on Lévi-Strauss says: 'Die sein Leben bestimmende Entdeckung war die Existenz einer unbekannten Grösse, die dem Bekannten seine Ordnung gibt, eines Unbewussten, das allem Bewussten Struktur verleiht, war die Erkenntnis, dass Wissenschaft heute darin bestehen müsste, dieses Unbekannte bekannter und das Unbewusste bewusster zu machen' (Schiwy, 1969: 37).

The conviction that religion should be studied as a function of culture is not meant as an attempt at reduction. It can never be the aim of science of religion to try to reduce religion to something else. It is only a protest against theological absolutism. V. Turner is quite right in stating: 'One has to consider religious phenomena in terms of religious ideas and doctrines, and not only, or principally in terms of disciplines which have arisen in connection with the study of secular institutions and processes. ... Religion is not determined by anything other than itself, though the religious finds expression in sensory phenomena' (Turner, 1969: 91 ff.). Reductionist theories of whatever kind give insufficient attention to the fact that for most religions the belief in the reality they postulate is essential for the consciousness of the large majority of all believers and thus for the religion in question itself. The remark made above about the relative value of religious self-understanding does not apply here: it is clear that most religions stand and fall with an effective belief in the beings and powers postulated by these religions as existing in an objective sense outside the mind of the believers.

2. Religion is a complex of notions, which as a rule form a more or less connected system, concerning man and world and in which an important function is given to one or more beings and/or powers, more or less different from human beings, as a rule of a superior quality, and which are generally referred to in explanations concerning the existence of the world and mankind, and those concerning life after death when this belief exists. The belief in the existence of these beings and/or powers influences those who believe in their existence.

These notions are mostly rather complicated and of great variability. The terminology used here is necessarily and deliberately rather vague. The term system is used more or less in its general significance, not in the strict sense some scholars prefer.

The fact that religious notions are mentioned first does not imply that religious notions in my opinion are necessarily antecedent or prior to religious behaviour etc. As a matter of fact it is quite clear that in most cases religious education starts with certain forms of behaviour and that the related notions are added later, and even then generally only up to a point. But the fact remains that, when asked, people as a rule do not say: I believe this because I act in this way, but conversely give a religious or ideological reason for their actions. Considered thus, notions have a certain right to be put first, if only as a didactic device.

3. This influence is expressed in notions, feelings, moods, behaviour, efforts, actions of the believers. There are two directions of expression:

a. Ritual actions, etc., concerned with and directed towards the above mentioned higher beings. These notions, etc., may be either collective or individual.

b. Social and ethical notions, etc., either collective or individual, concerned with and directed towards mankind and world.

Although a and b in most cases can be distinguished, the difference may be mainly one of manifest emphasis. It is not always possible to separate them because they may exist in combination. Moreover, notions which are, when acted out, manifestly ritual and directed towards higher beings act in fact on the congregation of believers, while social and ethical notions, when acted out, may be considered by the believers to influence those beings as well.

Religious notions are concerned with gods, etc., mankind and world. In the first case we may speak of theology, in the second of religious anthropology and in the third of religious cosmology. In some forms of religion metaphorical expression is more important than that in the form of ideas, but there is no essential difference between theological and mythological thinking. In mythological thinking the metaphorical character is paramount, in theology thinking in abstract concepts dominates. Apart from the question of principle whether theological thinking can exist that is not at least partly thinking in metaphors, and apart from the practical problem that it is often difficult in foreign cultures with foreign languages to distinguish clearly between metaphorical (mythical) thinking and theological thinking in ideas, we may be convinced that extreme forms are less common than mixed or intermediary ones.

As a rule there is also an emotional bond between the believers and their religions, although the degree of emotional concern may vary from culture to culture and from individual to individual.

Behaviour, efforts and action together constitute religious action.

4. Within the sphere of religious action two kinds may be distinguished:

a. Behaviour which can only be regarded as meaningful and fit to the purpose within the framework of a religion, or a group of religions, respectively all religions, i.e. by persons who either believe in a specific religion, or in the fundamentals of a group of religions or of all religions, or by those persons who are in any case willing to accept for a time, whatever their motivation may be, the expressions of one or more given religions as true. Thus it is possible for reasons of method to accept for a time the belief system of a religion as worthy of belief. This kind of religious action I call symbolic religious action. As B. Schneider explains: 'This emphasizes ... that 'means' and 'ends' are related by symbolic congruity or appropiateness, not by a causal nexus' (Schneider, 1970: 32).

b. Actions which can be regarded as meaningful and fit to the purpose in that function of culture which is called religion, and which in other functions of culture, such as e.g. natural sciences and technics, psychology and social sciences can also be so regarded, and that in the same manner as a religion regards them to be so.

Symbolic actions as such are, of course, not the exclusive prerogative of religion. By religious action I also understand all action caused and motivated by religion. The term religious action is not a value judgment. Both types of religious action need not be mutually exclusive. The restriction made concerning the actions mentioned under 4b, that they can be regarded as meaningful and fit to the purpose in other sections of culture, and that in the same manner as a religion regards them to be so, is not superfluous. Exact and technical science cannot accept praying as meaningful and fit to the purpose in solving a problem. Psychologically, however, or from the point of view of social science praying can be thus regarded, but these disciplines do not consider that it works in the same manner as religion supposes it to do.

5. To be able to speak of religion there should exist a group showing a minimum of institutionalization and a minimum of ritual forms.

This point is kept vague because no exact dividing lines can be given. The possibility of discussion on and difference of opinion about certain specific instances should be kept open.

6. It is acceptable to presume that religion is surrounded by an area of religiosity which exists apart from religion, but which under certain circumstances can lead to religion, or which may be a residue of religion.

The term religiosity is not ideal but is used here for lack of a better one.

7. The difference between religion and superstition is fluid and is determined by general cultural factors. Conceptions and actions, etc. resulting therefrom which can be considered as being in contradiction with the general world view of a specific culture or subculture and which lack the force to form a new religious community belong to the sector of superstition.

Some additional remarks may be made:

1. The beings and powers in which the adherents of a religion believe are different from human beings, but, apart from some rare exceptions, not totally different. Rudolf Otto, while theorizing about the Holy as the *ganz Andere*, has made the rare exceptions the general norm and has thus greatly impeded our understanding of religion as it actually is.

Although the question may be put as a matter of principle, whether man ever can have knowledge of a god who is totally different from man, we may concede that there are some instances, although rare, in which this limit has been closely approached. As a rule the situation is different, in some cases very much so.

According to the Kalabari Ijo (Southern Nigeria) people can increase a spirit's power by venerating it intensely and they are able to reduce its power to practically zero by neglecting it (Horton, 1965: 6). In Ceylon the majority of the population has two religions, a kind of Hinayana Buddhism and the cult of the prebuddhistic gods. As, according to the doctrines of Buddhism, gods are in a worse position than men with regard to their own ultimate salvation, human beings may sacrifice to the gods part of their own merit (Von Fürer-Haimendorf, 1967: 204ff.). Many other instances may be given; to quote only one more, there existed a ritual in Polynesia for chasing away a god as punishment for his negligence in helping man (Guiart, 1962: 98).

2. The term holy has a wider use than only the strictly religious one. Use of this term and related ones in other languages need not always necessarily imply that we are confronted with religious phenomena. This error has often been made with regard to *mana*. All religious terms are ultimately derived from non-religious ones.

3. There is a tendency to consider religion, experienced as confrontation with the ultimate, as a universal quality of all religions. This may be true in many cases but it is not necessarily so and belongs as a general statement to the sphere of belief or metaphysical ontology.

J. S. Helfer rightly says: 'Ultimacy is clearly a value category and cannot be justified other than in authoritarian fashion. Religious values are characteristically different from economic values, for example, but the assumption that their solipsistically determined ultimacy is descriptively arrived at cannot be substantiated (Helfer, 1968: 3ff.).

The way in which J. M. Kitagawa speaks about religion is a clear echo of a period of science of religion which held sway in the years between 1920 and 1945, but which now must make room for a new and different approach (Kitagawa, 1967: 39ff.).

4. The fact that there exists no known culture without religion does not necessarily imply that such a culture cannot exist.

5. When considering religion we must distinguish between three sectors or aspects. When we consider religion as a form of interaction between gods and men, the following aspects can and should be distinguished:

a. The direct human experience of, and man's reaction to an act of revelation. In some religions this aspect is emphasized in the sources, in some not.

b. The sharing of an experience as mentioned under a without having actually experienced it oneself.

c. The aspect of religion as a traditional cultural pattern.

The word revelation is used here as a term of science of religion and not at all as a theological term, as discussed at length in my doctoral thesis (Van Baaren, 1951).

6. It is advisable to make another distinction of religion into three sectors or aspects:

a. Religion as an individual and often intuitive way of experiencing reality, if integrated in or subordinated to a whole which may be called religion.

b. Religion as an intellectual system proposing views concerning world and man, and the rites etc. in connection with these views, if integrated in or subordinated to a whole which may be called religion.

c. A social and cultural phenomenon, comprising other social and cultural phenomena if and in as far as these are considered to be connected with religion, and all rites, etc. connected with this phenomenon, if integrated in or subordinated to a whole which may be called religion.

7. It is inadvisable to make a distinction in Dutch between *godsdienst* and *religie* as this is an artificial distinction for which the words needed are lacking in most languages.

8. The origin of religion has purposely been left out of discussion.

G.B. Vetter offers 32 theories concerning the origin and essence of religion (Vetter, 1958).

Science of religion differs from theology, especially from dogmatic theology, because it is limited to an empirical study of religions as they are, and because it does not acknowledge the authority of any religion to influence or determine the results of this research. In the same way this discipline also differs from the so-called *theologia religionum* (sometimes called religiology) which studies other religions in the light of the religion which is considered the true one and which judges other religions by standards belonging to that one religion. When Muslim theologians reproach Christianity with having abandoned monotheism for tritheism, this is a kind of *theologia religionum*. Science of religion does not claim for itself a higher content of truth than related disciplines. Dogmatic theology is essentially normative, or at least tending to normativity, because the truth of its own religion is one of its data. For the believing adherents of a religion, as a rule, their own religion forms the sacred model (the word used here in its everyday significance) as well *of the divine reality* as *for this reality*. In theory it is acceptable that one religion is true and all other religions untrue, but the truth or untruth of a religion can never be proven by accepting one religion as the standard of truth (Cf. Obbink, 1957: 10). The only thing which can sometimes be stated is that in a certain historical situation or social context one religion functions better than another one. For science of religion, however, all religions can only be human models of and for the reality of man and world in their totality, comprising as well the material reality as what we call immaterial or spiritual reality.

For the relation between theology and science of religion see also Rudolph (1962, 1967, 1968). J.S. Helfer criticizes succinctly and excellently the way in which certain prominent historians of religion succeed in considering Christianity either as the opposite or as the fulfilment of non-Christian religions. He mentions by name Otto, Van der Leeuw, Kraemer, Zaehner and Eliade (Helfer, 1968: 4-7). I. M. Lewis writing on ecstatic religions judges Zaehner: 'Indeed, only those who share his assurance will accept Zaehner's conclusion, that Christian mysticism represents a more lofty form of transcendental experience than any other' (Lewis, 1971: 23).

By confronting religion with the rest of the world in which we live, we can not only investigate what corrections this world needs to be in accordance with a given religious model, but also what corrections a given religious model needs to be able to keep on functioning in a changing historical situation (cf. Van Baaren, 1972).

The theological distinction between true and false religion makes no sense for science of religion.

This is not the same as the so-called phenomenological *epochè*, which will be treated later, according to which science of religion agrees to refrain from judgments relative to religious truth and value in the knowledge of its own limitations. This only makes sense for those who are convinced that it is possible to demonstrate scientifically the truth of a religion or of religion in general, or at least to demonstrate the probability of this truth. The truth of religion as considered in dogmatics belongs to a different linguistic game and all considerations of this kind should be eliminated from the fundamental rules of science of religion.

Many departments of theology (e.g. Old Testament, New Testament, Church History) can be studied according to the rules of science of religion and should in that case be considered to be part of this discipline. Philosophy of religion is a different discipline which cannot be assimilated by science of religion as defined in this paper.

Many scholars distinguish within science of religion a number of departments; especially four of these are often mentioned:
1. History of religions;
2. Science of religion as a systematic discipline, often called phenomenology or comparative religion;
3. Psychology of religion;
4. Sociology of religion.

Although this division is practicable, and therefore used here, it has no systematic value.

History of religions is nothing else than a part of history and psychology and sociology of religion are nothing but psychology and sociology applied to religion. Many other disciplines can usefully be applied to the study of religions, e.g. psychiatry, economics, art history etc. It would in all these cases be better to speak of different approaches to the study of religion than of separate disciplines. Only the systematic study of religion, whatever name we give it, is a separate discipline based on all the relevant approaches of other disciplines, but not limited to those.

History of religions is a department of history and uses the same methods and means as all other historical research.

The methods used in history need not be discussed here. See for a clear and succinct treatment M. Smith 1968. See also Drijvers in this volume. The distinction made in some theological circles between *Geschichte* and *Historie* makes no sense whatever.

History of religions can be divided into special and general history of religions. Special history of religions treats historically limited subjects, e.g. Roman or Egyptian religion, or the history of sacrifice in the ancient Near East or that of mysticism in India. The religion of Israel and Christianity form part of the material studied by history of religions and they should be studied according to the same methods as all other religions. Only their special importance for the Christian Churches gives them an exceptional place in the Christian world. In the same way Islam takes a special place in the Muslim world.

The ideal of general history of religions is to write a history of religion as such. Lack of material makes this impossible. It is, however, from time to time worth trying to give a synthesis of all knowledge collected by history of religions.

Systematic science of religion has been founded by P.D. Chantepie de la Saussaye (1887). Significant in Holland for the evolution of this discipline was the work of W.B. Kristensen and G. van der Leeuw. The second, with Rudolf Otto, largely determined the form this discipline took between 1920 and 1940. Their combined influence is still strong.

The Dutch scholars mentioned called this discipline phenomenology. K. Goldammer makes a distinction between phenomenology and *systematische Religionswissenschaft* (Goldammer, 1960), thus continuing a discussion by J. Wach (1924).

Science of religion as a systematic discipline is based on the material collected by history, sociology, anthropology, psychology, etc., and tries to classify these materials systematically, to understand and to explain them. Van der Leeuw and others state that this discipline only aims at finding relations which can be understood intuitively, but thus science of religion is fettered by an intuitive method, the heuristic value of which may be great, but the results of which cannot be verified. The exclusive opposition often made between understanding and explaining leads to confusion: all understanding is a form of explaining and the other way round.

In science understanding can only be used as a special form of explaining. It is a subjective form of explaining in which a subject aims at finding clarity concerning an object by trying to give it a place in his own personal pattern of thinking, feeling and experiencing. The knowledge arrived at in this way is no valid form of science, its scientific exactness or falsity has to be demonstrated and checked by scientific methods.

See for understanding and explaining the excellent discussion in F. Sierksma (1951).

Science of religion as a systematic discipline has been given many other names apart from phenomenology. H. Frick called it typology (Frick, 1928).

The term phenomenology, used by Van der Leeuw and others, was an unfortunate choice and elicited much misunderstanding. Its connection with the philosophical phenomenology of E. Husserl and his school was never more than superficial at best. This has been explicitly pointed out by C.J. Bleeker and Th.P.van Baaren (Bleeker, *Structuur*: 19; Van Baaren, 1960b, 6). If we want to preserve the term phenomenology, we must indicate its exact relationship to philosophical phenomenology. In England and America many scholars used to speak of Comparative Religion, a less objectionable term, but rather one-sided because it stresses the element of comparing and neglects others. See for the phenomenological method in the study of religions Eva Hirschmann (1940).

The term phenomenology is also too restricted. The discipline I have in mind does not only study religious phenomena, but also the human beings in whom these phenomena become manifest and the religions both separately and in their totality and in their mutual relations as well.

I prefer the name of science of religion as a systematic discipline (for short systematic science of religion). This term is coined in analogy with and in opposition to systematic theology.

It is often argued that religions cannot be mutually compared, and that especially Christianity cannot be compared with other religions. This argument as a rule more or less clearly betrays an apologetic concern. Each religion is as such historically unique, but all religions are built up out of the same basic elements. There are probably not very many of these basic elements, which makes it a legitimate form of research to compare all religions. Comparison, however, does not mean equalizing. There are, of course, also many historic relationships, dependencies and interdependencies which make comparison not only feasible but even obligatory.

In analogy to Heisenberg's celebrated principle of uncertainty in exact sciences, we may acknowledge that science of religion needs a comparable principle of uncertainty: each religion is unique and comparable at one and the same time, depending on the point of view taken.

There is no reason for science of religion to treat any religion as essentially different from the others. This, of course, does not exclude the legitimacy of the believer's claim that his own religion is the one and only true one. This claim, in fact only made by a restricted number of religions, is of no relevance for science of religion.

Comparison of religions is made difficult in practice because the various elements which make up a religion are not static, not unchangeable and not separated by water-tight compartments, but are contained in a dynamic system of relations, influencing each other mutually and at the same time influenced by the religion as a whole. From this results a complicated feed-back mechanism.

It is for this reason that, according to my opinion, it is impossible to determine the essence of a religion by indicating one or a few essential elements. The character of a religion is rather determined by the importance of the various elements, by the way in which they are related and co-operate and by the structural form of the whole. This can only be expressed by using a not too short circumstantial description (cf. Van Baaren, 1967). We may go one step further and state that science of religion is not concerned with discovering the essence of *the* or *a* religion; this is a task of philosophy or theology.

A short circumscription can only indicate a few dominant elements of a given religion and is usually worse than useless, to wit misleading (cf. Van der Leeuw, 1956: 704-743).

Systematic science of religion is no historical discipline as history of religions is; it is a systematic one. It is distinguished from other systematic disciplines taught in the faculty of theology by its lack of a normative character. It only studies religions as they are empirically and disclaims any statements concerning the value and truth of the phenomena studied. This does not imply that the student of this discipline is not allowed to entertain normative conceptions as a person, it only means that he acknowledges that those convictions are irrelevant for his scientific work and that he must rule them out as much as possible in his research.

This means in any case that they have no claim to function in his methodology.

It is often said that the student of religion should be a man of faith himself; experience, however, seems to indicate that intensive partisanship for or against a religion or religion in general harms the objectivity of research. Helfer expresses this objection clearly and wittily: 'Strangely, but appropiately, economic historians are not more "economic", military historians are not more "militant", intellectual historians are not more "intellectual", or social historians more "social"; why must historians of religions persist in being more "religious"?' (Helfer, 1968: 7).

This, of course, does not detract from the value of a certain congeniality between the researcher and the material he studies, but this same congeniality may be present in those who attack religion. It is a commonplace that the enemy's eye is often sharper than that of a friend.

As the truth of religion cannot be scientifically demonstrated, science of religion refrains from any judgment in this matter. This is not the same as what van der Leeuw calls *epochè* with a Greek term derived from Husserl's phenomenology. Van der Leeuw uses this term to indicate a modest suspension of judgment. The scientific validity of theological statements is kept fully intact, it is only for the time being put in brackets (*eingeklammert*) (Van der Leeuw, 1956: 774ff.). The point of view defended here is not that theological pronouncements concerning the truth or untruth of a religion should be put between brackets for the time being, but that they should be crossed out definitively from the language of science of religion as irrelevant. The same, of course, is true of all anti-theological pronouncements in the same matter. It is self-evident that this does not exclude the relevancy of this kind of pronouncements in the world of belief or unbelief.

While the discussion about the truth of religion can be eliminated from science of religion, the problem of religious values is a different one. According to U. Bianchi value judgements belong legitimately to science of religion (Bianchi, 1964). This is a problem which needs further research. It may be possible to form value judgments based on norms acknowledged by the religion judged. Value judgments derived from other religions than the religion judged are not applicable (Van Baaren, 1960b: 8).

Science of religion in all its forms consists of describing, classifying and explaining the material studied, and if need be of understanding it. The first three terms are self-evident, but the last one needs some commentary, the more so because this aspect has been singled out as the essential one by some schools of science of religion. If we agree with van der Leeuw that understanding is 'Die *Einschaltung* des Phänomens *in das eigene Leben*', it is clear that we have progressed beyond the possibilities of science of religion as proposed in this paper. Understanding may be a fruitful addition to the scientific study of the material available, but understanding as defined by van der Leeuw is too subjective to be used as a valid argument in scientific research.

Influenced by the neo-romantic ideas of Dilthey, etc. especially Van der Leeuw has reduced science of religion to a form of understanding, thus making this discipline into a subjective form of art (cf. Sierksma, 1951: 28-69). However, as mentioned already, it is wrong to consider explaining and understanding as two contradictory concepts. There is no explaining without a measure of understanding and no understanding without explaining. It is certainly not true that understanding as such gives us a deeper knowledge of religion than explaining. It is true, however, that understanding can have a didactic value for the student. See for an extreme expression of the value of *Verstehen*, e.g. Schilling (1957) in which understanding is stressed in a way that renders it absurd in any form of scholarly research.

Intuition is certainly important, but appeal to it is not an argument in any scientific discussion. Intuition may have an important heuristic value and the *Verstehende Schule* adds an aesthetic dimension which has an importance of its own, but which cannot be made operational in scientific research. The results of the *verstehende* method are never verifiable.

Van der Leeuw was very much conscious of these dangers: 'Es ist dieses Erleben allerdings mehr eine Kunst als eine Wissenschaft' (Van der Leeuw, 1956: 773). And a few pages later he writes: 'Soll die Phänomenologie ihre Aufgabe vollbringen, so hat sie immerwährende Korrektur der gewissenhaftesten philologischen, archäologischen Forschung sehr nötig' (Van der Leeuw, 1956: 776). Why Van der Leeuw himself transgressed these rules so frequently can only be solved by a study in depth of his life and work. A partial answer is given by the sentence following the second quotation: 'Nicht als ginge die sachliche Verarbeitung dieses Tatsachenmaterials ohne Deutung, d.h. ohne Phänomenologie vonstatten' (Van der Leeuw, 1956: 776). This is in my opinion an indication of insufficient insight in the diverse cognitive value of methods of acquiring knowledge. If other disciplines also 'deuten' their facts, this may easily lead to the conviction that the student of phenomenology is hardly concerned with their interpretations, because he does this much better. Van der Leeuw, however, knew this danger very well; according to him phenomenology becomes 'zur reinen Kunst oder zur leeren Phantastik, sobald sie sich der Kontrolle durch die philologisch-archäologischen Deutung entzieht' (Van der Leeuw, 1956: 777).

Starting from the contrast between the concepts of type and of object, F. Helwig expresses well-founded criticism of phenomenology as method, summarized in the statement that the so-called *Wesensschau* is not concerned 'with what is objective in a factual sense, but with the image which is experienced in the imagination' (Helwig, 1967: 171ff.).

Science of religion is not more subjective than other so-called *Geisteswissenschaften*; it aims at reaching a maximum of objectivity and a minimum of subjectivity.

He who thinks that objectivity is completely impossible in this type of scientific discipline, may use impartiality instead. See the dialogue between H. Kraemer and Th.P. van Baaren on this subject (Kraemer, 1959; Van Baaren, 1960-1961; Kraemer, 1961-1962; Van Baaren, 1961-1962; De Vos, 1962: 86-90).

There always exists a tension between the objectivity aimed at and the inevitable subjective factors.

Helfer makes some lucid remarks concerning the problem of subjectivity being related to the fact that science of religion, like other comparable disciplines, is 'grounded in an hermeneutic situation: that is in an interpretative framework which establishes the possibilities and limits of critical analysis and creative synthesis' (Helfer, 1968: 1).

In phenomenology of religion it was allowed to divorce religious phenomena from their cultural milieu. This proceeding, which prohibits all understanding, has often been rightly attacked. Systematic science of religion should avoid this erroneous method as much as possible.

The following, said about Gnosticism, is valid for all religions: Gnosticism is a 'historic complex that cannot be satisfactorily analysed simply by resolving it into its elements. The method of addition and subtraction does not work in the history of religions. A religion cannot be compared to a collection of coins to which one can add a few or from which one can take some without causing some essential change. A religion, like a molecule, has a structure in which every element has only one possible place; add one, subtract one, even only change the place of some of the elements, and the result can be a decided and essential transformation. Gnosticism is what it is, because of the manner in which a considerable number of elements together form an organic whole, and because of the way in which every one of these elements functions in the whole complex. As such Gnosticism is a unique historic phenomenon and can only be described as such' (Van Baaren, 1967: 175). If I were writing the same thing now, I would avoid the term 'organic' which is apt to be misleading. K. Lewin's field theory may be of great use here (cf. Leertouwer, Chapter 4, in this volume).

Reflections like those above can give rise to the application of structuralistic methods. If it is true, as I think, that the various religions are all built up out of a restricted number of elementary basic structures, we must explain the large diversity of religions by the various combinations of these structures. This point of view may clarify the discussion about the possibility of comparing religions.

Only few comparative studies meet the methodical demands which may reasonably be made.

In the field of science of religion a first beginning has been made by H. Frick by his distinction between homologous and analogous phenomena. Homologous phenomena resemble each other structurally but function differently, analogous phenomena are structurally different but exercise the same functions. The example worked out by Frick has become famous. In Buddhism, Christianity and Islam the founders are homologous, but the function of Christ in Christianity is analogous to that of the doctrine (*dharma*) in Buddhism and that of the Koran in Islam (Frick, 1928: 16).

Social sciences have done far more work in this field, but much still remains to be done. See for an attempt to apply these insights to the study of religions e.g. Van Beek, *Drie religies*. One of the main future tasks of our research group will be to test and to work out new methods of comparison, not only between different religions but also between different kinds of source material, for instance, between textual and iconographical material.

One of the questions which must be necessarily solved to be able to make valid comparisons is that concerning primary and secondary elements or, to phrase it differently, which elements should be considered functions of other more elementary ones. Thus, for instance, the divine attributes of omniscience and all-seeingness in Christianity and Islam are no elementary data, but derive from, are functions of the extremely large distance between God and men in both these religions. As long as the gods live more or less in the same space as humankind man has no need of omniscient and all-seeing gods. The need to attribute these qualities to the gods or to God only arises when the distance between the two has become unbridgeably large. Thinking further in this direction, the question may be put whether it is true that a god is omniscient and allseeing, because he is considered to be a god of the sun or of the heavens, as many think, or whether it is not rather the other way round that in fact a god becomes a god of the sun or of the heavens, because he is first considered as all-seeing, etc. This remark touches on an important problem in connection with the origin of religion which is often sought in the experience of nature.

In many cases, of course, it is clear that nature has been the direct model for religious image-forming and reflection. The Kalabari Ijo (Southern Nigeria) who live in a swampy region picture the many twisting creeks of their country as gigantic snakes and know myths in which the origin of these creeks is derived from mythical snakes (Horton, 1962: 202).

Psychology and sociology of religion, as has been mentioned already, are nothing but psychology and sociology applied to religion. They have no methods which belong exclusively to psychology or sociology of religion. Many other disciplines should be related to the studyof religion, two obvious choices are economy and psychiatry. Another obvious choice is art history.

Most handbooks of phenomenology neglect the aspect of art, although Van der Leeuw pioneered in this field; unfortunately insufficient knowledge of the material, except in the case of music, and a too exclusively theological point of view made his researches in this field of little use for science of religion (Van der Leeuw, 1932). F. Sierksma in two of his books has shown new ways (Sierksma, 1962: 1966). See for the restricted field of primitive art Van Baaren (1962), and many excellent field studies of cultural and social anthropologists. Some attention is paid to art by K. Goldammer (1960).

The terminology of science of religion is still unsatisfactory. The two main objections are:

1. The terminology in use is insufficiently exact. The term ancestor cult, to give an example, is used for all forms in which ancestors receive some kind of recognition or cult. The term ancestor cult should be reserved for one special form. About the term ancestor statues or ancestor images the same thing can be said. This inexact terminology invites confusion and misunderstanding.

See for a concrete example concerning ancestor cult. e.g. Bradbury (1966). See for an attempt at a further classification of ancestor statues Van Baaren (1968:20).

2. Many of the terms used are derived from specific religions and have been generalized and applied to all religions and to religion in general, thus e.g. the tarm *taboo*, as if we had to do with identical phenomena the whole world over, instead of with conceptions which may be roughly comparable but which convey in each culture a number of specific additional notions, while in other cultures at least part of these additional notions may be completely different. By generalizing these terms we give the additional notions with the culture from which we derive the term a quasi-universal significance and validity. These terms have not been coined to indicate religious phenomena in general, but to express a specific notion in a specific culture.

If we reflect on the terminology of science of religion, some terms will soon appear superfluous, as, for instance, the term *mana* which has given rise to so much misunderstanding that it seems to be wisest to abandon it except in some very specific context. The same is true for the term *taboo* and for many other terms like *totem*, *dema*, etc. Some terms may perhaps be retained in a very specific and restricted meaning.

To give an example, J. Maes has proposed to define fetish as a statue or object that is given significance and value by certain elements added to the statue or object by a priest or other religious functionary (Maes, 1935). Even then it may be advisable to abandon this term, because of the popular use that has been made of it.

There are two ways open to us:

1. We can use for each culture the term used by that culture itself. Then we should, when speaking of *taboo*, use for Hawaii the term *kapu*, for New Zealand and a number of other islands *tapu*, for the Northern Solomons *tambu*, etc. But then we must also use *pali* for Borneo, *fady* for Madagascar, etc. For special studies concerning one region, or some cultures which are closely related, this is advisable, but for systematic science of religion this would lead to a chaos of terms in which it soon becomes impossible to find one's way.

2. We can try to give each phenomenon a name which fits it as objectively and clearly as possible. Such terms can only be found by a

thorough analysis of the many comparable but not identical phenomena which we find in our source material. We must try to find a term which is as exact as possible and which occasions no terminological mystification. Thus we can replace the term *taboo* which is inexact, gives rise to misunderstanding and occasions mystification by the term ritual injunction. Within the category of ritual injunctions further subcategories may be distinguished. We can then replace the term *taboo* sign by injunction emblem (Brain-Pollock, 1971: 16).

A term derived from our own culture is in case of need preferable to a term derived from a foreign culture. In the second case we operate with two unknown quantities, in the first case only one. In this way we can use the term revelation as a *terminus technicus* of science of religion (Van Baaren, 1951).

REFERENCES

Van Baaren, Th. P. (1951), *Voorstellingen van openbaring phaenomenologisch beschouwd*, diss. Utrecht.
— (1960a), *Wij Mensen, Religie en wereldbeschouwing bij schriftloze volken*. Utrecht, J. Bijleveld.
— (1960b), *Doolhof der goden*. Amsterdam, Querido.
— (1962), *Bezielend beelden, Inleiding tot de beeldende kunst der primitieve volken*. Amsterdam, Querido.
— (1967), 'Towards a definition of Gnosticism', *Studies in the History of Religions*, XII: *Le origini dello Gnosticismo*, Colloquio di Messina 13-18 Aprile 1966, Ed. Ugo Bianchi. Leiden, Brill.
   (1968), *Korwars and Korwar style, Art and ancestor worship in Northwest New Guinea*. The Hague-Paris, Mouton.
— (1969), 'Systematische Religionswissenschaft', *Nederlands Theologisch Tijdschrift* (Wageningen, Veenman), 24 (1969-1970) pp. 81-88.
— (1972), 'The flexibility of myth,' *Ex orbe religionum, Studia Geo Widengren oblata II*, pp. 199-206. Leiden, Brill.
Van Beek,W. E. A. (no year), 'Drie religies, een vergelijking,' *Mededelingen van het Instituut voor Culturele Anthropologie der Rijksuniversiteit te Utrecht*. Utrecht, Instituut voor Culturele Anthropologie.
Bianchi, Ugo (1964), *Probleme der Religionsgeschichte*, Göttingen, Vandenhoeck und Ruprecht.

Bleeker, C.J. (no year), *De structuur van de godsdienst*. Den Haag, Servire.
Bradbury, R.E. (1966), 'Fathers, elders and ghosts in Edo religion,' in Michael Banton (ed.), *Anthropological approaches to the study of religion*. London, Tavistock Publications.
Brain, Robert, and Pollock, Adam (1971), *Bangwa funerary sculpture*. London, Gerald Duckworth and Co.
Chantepie de la Saussaye, P.D. (1887/9), *Lehrbuch der Religionsgeschichte*, I:1887, II:1889, Freiburg i. Br., Akademische Verlagsbuchhandlung von J.C.B. Mohr (Paul Siebeck).
Frick, H. (1928), *Vergleichende Religionswissenschaft*. Berlin-Leipzig, Walter de Gruyter & Co.
Von Fürer-Haimendorf, C. (1967), *Morals and merit*. London, Weidenfeld and Nicholson.
Geertz, C. (1966), 'Religion as a cultural system,' in Michael Banton (ed.), *Anthropological approaches to the study of religion*. London, Tavistock Publications.
Goldammer, K. (1960), *Die Formenwelt des Religiösen*. Stuttgart, Alfred Kröner Verlag.
Guiart, J. (1962), *Les religions de l'Océanie*. Paris, Presses Universitaires de France.
Hardt (1966), *Social anthropology*, 2. ed. Oxford, Oxford University Press.
Helfer, James S., ed. (1968), *On method in the history of religions*. Middletown, Wesleyan University Press.
Helwig, P. (1967), *Karakterologie*. Utrecht-Antwerpen, Spectrum (Prisma).
Hirschmann, Eva (1940), *Phänomenologie der Religion, eine historisch-systematische Untersuchung von 'Religionsphänomenologie' und 'religionsphänomenologischer Methode' in der Religionswissenschaft*. Würzburg, Verlag Aumuhle.
Horton, Robin (1962), 'The Kalabari Ijo,' *Africa*, XXXII, 1962.
— (1965), *Kalabari sculpture*. Apapa, Nigerian National Press.
Kitagawa, J.M. (1967), 'Primitive, classical and modern religions: A perspective on understanding the history of religions,' *The History of Religions, essays on the problem of understanding*. Chicago-London, The University of Chicago Press.
Kristensen, W.B. (1960), *The meaning of religion*. The Hague, Martinus Nijhoff.
Van der Leeuw, G. (1932), *Wegen en grenzen*. Amsterdam, H.J. Paris (2. dr. 1948).
— (1956), *Phänomenologie der Religion*, 2. Aufl. Tübingen, J.C.B. Mohr (Paul Siebeck).
Lewis, I.M. (1971), *Ecstatic religion*. Harmondsworth, Penguin Books.

Maes, J. (1935), *Fetischen of tooverbeelden uit Kongo*. Brussel, Annales du Musée du Congo Belge, Tervueren.

Norbeck, E. (1961), *Religion in primitive society*. New York, Harper & Brothers.

Obbink, H. W. (1957), 'Enige kanttekeningen bij het vraagstuk van de religieuze tolerantie,' Ter herdenking van de 321e Dies Natalis der Rijksuniversiteit Utrecht, Utrecht.

Rudolph, K. (1962), *Die Religionsgeschichte an der Leipziger Universität und die Entwicklung der Religionswissenschaft*. Berlin, Akademie Verlag.

— (1967), 'Die Problematik der Religionswissenschaft als akademisches Lehrfach,' *Kairos*, IX, pp. 22-42.

— (1968), 'Zur Problematik der Religionswissenschaft,' *Kairos*, X, pp. 290-291.

Schiwy, G. (1969), *Der französische Strukturalismus, Mode, Methode, Ideologie*. Hamburg, Rowohlt.

Schneider, L. (1970), *Sociological approach to religion*. New York, John Wiley & Sons.

Sierksma, F. (1951), *Freud, Jung en de religie*. Assen, Van Gorcum & Comp.

— (1960), *De mens en zijn goden*. Amsterdam, Djambatan.

— (1966), *Tibet's terrifying deities, sex and aggression in religious acculturation*. The Hague-Paris, Mouton.

Smith, M. (1968), 'Historical method in the study of religion,' in James S. Helfer (ed.), *On method in the history of religion*. Middletown, Wesleyan University Press.

Spiro, Melford E. (1966), 'Religion: Problems of Definition and Explanation,' in Michael Banton (ed.), *Anthropological approaches to the study of religion*. London, Tavistock Publications.

Swanson, G. E. (1968), *The birth of the gods*. Ann Arbor, University of Michigan Press.

Turner, V. W. (1969), *Chihamba, the White Spirit, a ritual drama of the Ndembu*. Manchester, Manchester University Press.

Vetter, G. B. (1958), *Magic and religion, their psychological nature, origin and function*. New York, Philosophical Library.

Wach, Joachim (1924), *Religionswissenschaft, Prolegomena zu ihrer wissenschaftstheoretischen Grundlegung*. Leipzig, Verlag der J. C. Henrichs'schen Buchhandlung.

Theory Formation in Science of Religion and the Study of the History of Religions

Van Baaren's Introduction 'Science of religion as a systematic discipline' rightly begins with a description of the phenomenon of religion as a component of culture, interacting with other component parts of the same culture. The advantage of this description is on the one hand that it is fairly circumstantial, so that a clearer demarcation can be drawn between that which forms the study of science of religion and other cultural phenomena, and on the other that it is free of value judgements, through the absence of such terms as 'essence of religion' or 'ultimate concern'. For definitions or descriptions of religion using these onto- logical terms are methodologically useless, since they are no more than 'definitional tautologies' (Baird, 1968: 25), which cannot be made operational. Not that Baird himself escaped this danger, for he introduces the concept 'ultimate concern' (Baird, 1968: 19, 21; 1971: 18) describing it as *a concern which is more important than anything else in the universe for the person involved*'. To such a pronouncement we may apply the words of J.S.Helfer, as quoted by Van Baaren: 'Ultimacy is clearly a value category and cannot be justified other than in an authoritarian fashion.'

Starting from this description, science of religion approaches the phenomenon of religion in its specific quality as well as in connexion with other cultural phenomena, while general and particular aspects of religion supplement one another as each presupposes the other. There is a need of theory to formalize the interrelation between the various com- ponents of a culture and present this in a model or models in such a way that problems may be formulated on that basis for application to the object or material under examination. Various consequences follow from the above for the practice of the four traditional branches of science of religion that Van Baaren names, viz.

1. History of religion;
2. Systematic or comparative science of religion;
3. Psychology of religion;
4. Sociology of religion.

History, psychology and sociology of religion cannot then be studied by themselves, but only in the respective framework of cultural history or social history, psychology and the behavioural sciences and social and cultural anthropology, which study the relation of man to his social context. Systematic or comparative science of religion can only begin its work after history of religion as well as psychology and sociology of religion have gathered sufficient material from various cultures and periods for comparison and systematization to be possible. These should not, however, be an end in themselves, for instance in order to arrive at some all-embracing description or definition of religion as the final goal of science of religion, as formulated by C. J. Bleeker: 'The student of the history of religions starts his study with an intuitive, hardly formulated, axiomatic notion of what religion is. His ultimate aim is an inclusive formulation of the essence of religion. Such a definition is the crowning of the whole work!' (cited by Baird, 1968: 23 ff.). Formalization and systematization must serve to elucidate historical, psychological and social phenomena and to provide a feed-back to the description that was used as a starting-point and may need correction, which may again lead to new questions. The primacy of theory does not therefore rest on substance, but is merely operational, in order to understand and explain cultural phenomena as well as possible so as to contribute to our knowledge of man.

It would seem that Van Baaren has not fully realized the implications of his own theoretical construct, especially with regard to history of religion, when he says that history of religion works with the same methods and aids as other historical disciplines, and then refers to the work of M. Smith for the historical method and its application to the study of religion. For *the* historical method does not exist; there are only methods, which are used in the discipline of history in accordance with the problem from which the researcher takes his start and the subject he is working on. 'The day of a single methodology in history, if it ever existed, is at any rate now gone' (Aydelotte, 1969: 4). The difficulties that crop up here can be apprehended when one reads the last sentence of M. Smith's essay: 'the historian, like the critic, must then be able to return from the world of imagination to that of fact, and to determine the relation of the poetic or religious complex to its environment in the historical world' (Smith, 1968: 16). What are 'facts' here, and what are these 'relations' to *which* other phenomena in the 'environment in the historical world'? The great problem in every sociological and historical approach to the phenomenon of religion shows up here: Is religion a meta-social datum, consisting of a complex of conceptions to which man gives an inward meaning, realizing it in his social, i.e. historical actions, or are religious conceptions a reflection of the social order? (cf. Kippenberg, 1971: 59, 81). In his contribution to the present volume, Leertouwer has pointed out that Van Baaren's description of religion inclines to assign a dominant place to conceptions, so that religious behaviour is in danger of exclusion. In historical research we have to do particularly with the interaction of religious conceptions and human actions. When Van Baaren describes religion as a function of culture, then the mutual relation of the various components of a culture becomes highly important, and also their interaction as demonstrated in human behaviour. It is upon this point that further research is required (cf. Kippenberg, 1971: 81), since we may wonder whether the aforesaid two ways of approach of sociology of religion, whereby either the religious conceptions or the social order are in turn dominant and determinant, do not land us in a cul-de-sac with two contestant parties endlessly repeating 'it is!' and 'it isn't!' An attempt might well be considered to apply Kurt Lewin's 'field theory' to historical material also, since it has produced very good results in cultural anthropology (cf. Leertouwer, Chap. 4, in this volume).

It is striking and indeed regrettable that there is little sign of the envisaging of such problems in recent handbooks of religious history, however excellently they may group a quantity of data. The recent *Historia Religionum* (1969) has in the Preface a basic scheme which was given to all the authors for treating the subject entrusted to them. This scheme is as follows:

1. Short Description of the Essence of the Religion;
2. Historical Development;

3. Conception of the Deity;
4. Worship;
5. Conception of Man.

One finds that most authors were unable to do anything with the Essence of the Religion or merely set down generalities, that the description of the Historical Development is quite short and that the myths, rites and theological conceptions are described in an a-historical, almost timeless way. The editors express the hope that in following this method of work 'structural similarities' between the religions will appear, showing the 'ideological parallelism' in the function of the various religions. Yet has not the material here been forced into a predetermined shape, on the unspoken and quite mistaken supposition that religions have the same function in all cultures? When attention is paid to the interaction of the various components of a culture, it is found that the various problems of life with which man is confronted are solved differently in different cultures. Cultural and social oppression, for instance, may lead to an explosion in acute Messianic movements or Cargo-cults, but such need not be the case. The relation of the religion to the social pattern of the culture concerned is decisive here (cf. Kippenberg, 1971: 68-73, and the literature cited there).

From another approach than Van Baaren's, from that of Hubbeling ('Theology, philosophy and science of religion and their logical and empirical presuppositions'), we also arrive at questions of historical discipline. After Hubbeling's disquisition on the various forms of logic he comes to science of religion and noted that classical logic is sufficient for it, but that there is a special need for 'a theory of probability in history'. However, before we are able to weigh argument, individually or in series, we must know what facts and therefore what arguments may or may not be brought into the discussion founded on a theoretical model. Thus we are again faced with questions regarding religion as a component of culture and the relation between religion and the other components of a culture. What we need most of all is a philosophy of science capable of assembling the relation of the various approaches to a single phenomenon in a serviceable model.

These problems are in part linked with the history of the historical discipline itself. Its character was formed mainly in the 19th century, when it flourished greatly. Its relation with literature, of old very close, (Schiller!), was the cause that historical works were a form of 'story-telling', so that the difference between history and historical novel was often slight. As a consequence, many historians regarded a description of the facts as tantamount to an explanation, so that there was often no stimulus to further analysis. The same century is also responsible for the tribal idols of the historians, viz. the dominant standing of political history (*l'idole politique*), the glorification of individuals (*l'idole individuelle*) and the craving always to study the development of things, and particularly their beginning (*l'idole chronologique*). Clearly there are links here with the strong nationalism in that century on the one hand, and on the other the unchecked foisoning of the comparative method that sought the primeval stage of everything (*Ursprache, Ureigentum,* Darwin's *Origin of Species* etc.). These idols of the historian, together with an imperfect method addicted to impressionistic generalizations such as 'spirit of the times', 'national character' (Metzger, 1963) and so on, an argumentation of frequently greater psychological than logical force, and selection of the material on subjective grounds and not in relation to a particular problem, also exerted their influence upon the historians of religion. The dividing of history into periods according to political events has usually been taken over in history of religions, e.g. in that of Egypt, the Roman empire and Islam. The great interest in political events and prominent individuals has led to numerous monographs on individual gods and founders of religion. Evolutionism has had an immense influence on the history of religions (Rudolph, 1971: 95-103), and so one might enumerate much else.

Another difficulty in studying history, and also history of religions, is the great predilection for written sources, and the consequent use that is made of earlier work. Cochran calls this 'the tyranny of persuasive rhetoric' (Cochran-Hofstadter, 1956), which leads to a continual re-grouping and perhaps supplementing of the available material, while the same set formula still conveys the problem. It is extremely difficult, working in this way, to introduce new problematic approaches in the study of history. Probably no discipline in the *universitas scientiarum* is more firmly tied down to its own past, and in no other is the function of written sources so dominant in bringing the silent past to indirect speech.

For the historian of religion studying a particular period, people or region, the application of the above is even more pressing. Just like the student of ancient history, for instance, the historian of religions is as a rule not a professional historian, but a philologist or a theologian with a special interest. Discussions of methodical problems in the wide field of general history usually pass him by, so that they do not influence the problematical approaches in his discipline (Finley, 1963: 31 ff.). This relative isolation is reinforced by a general dislike of applying theories derived from other disciplines in the field of historical research in religion. As a rule the results of the work of, for instance, Robertson Smith, Sir James Frazer and Jane Harrison are simply set aside as non-valid, without any admission that the *Anliegen* of these scholars is perfectly legitimate. An extreme form of this attitude is seen in the vindication of a private autonomous subject of history of religions, viz. the religions, for the study of which the discipline possesses an autonomous method of its own. History of religions and history of culture are then seen as clearly differentiated fields, so that A. Brelich, the defender of this view, can say of the historian of religions: 'Ce qui est important, c'est qu'il étudie cette religion en historien des religions, et non en historien de cette civilisation; que sa problématique et sa méthode soient celles de l'histoire des religions; ...' (1970: 58).

As a historical discipline science of religions does not differ from other subdivisions of the science of history as regards its method of working. Usually there are four stages:

1. Examination of the facts on the basis of the available data;
2. Formulating an explanatory hypothesis;
3. Analysis of the implications of this hypothesis;
4. Checking these implications by means of additional data.

For every interpretation of data a theory is needed; this holds good for the setting up of the problem, for the ordering of the data found, for the formulating of an hypothesis as well as for the whole process of argumentation, so that the function of theory in the science of history and consequently in history of religions is the same as in other sciences, that is to supply questions to the researcher whereby information is turned into data that can be used scientifically. For that which takes place in the continuous course of historical time has no ratio in itself. The researcher brings structure into the historical happening, so that its elements and aspects come into a rational causal connexion and become comprehensible and explicable. For this, a theory is required to mark off a field of research, state what may be found there and which aspects thereof are essential. Armed with such a theory the researcher goes to work. Even the collector of historical facts works with a theory, sometimes unconsciously, that gives direction to his work. Historical material comprises far more than facts. Often it is an amorphous, unstructured happening presented piece-meal in information regarding many different events that may be connected. In scientific practice then, to collect facts is to pick up data from their context, to generalize and to select, after which the facts are sometimes used in quite a different connexion. Isolated facts have little historical value. 'The most challenging problem of research is often not to collect or recite the evidence but to display the context in which it is significant, to show how results that are trivial or meaningless in one frame of reference may become useful or even decisive in another' (Aydelotte, 1963: 167). A theory, then, has the heuristic function of making events comprehensible and explicable, and therefore we often need more theories to approximate to reality, and these theories must not be too comprehensive to be workable. For in historical science as in the social sciences what we seek is 'knowledge of what is' and not 'knowledge of what should be', to introduce the Weberian distinction between different kinds of knowledge (cf. McGrew, 1958: 280). All-embracing theories are only too apt to pass for reality itself, as depicting all that happens in the world in a single consistent theory that explains every fact. Such theories, however inspiring, no longer have any heuristic value; they cannot be made to work. The reification of concepts causes 'knowledge of what is' to pass into 'knowledge of what should be' and the examples of this are legion. Toynbee's and Sorokin's theories are good examples in the field of general history, and dynamistic or animistic theories or concepts of 'ultimate concern' and similar phenomena in science of religion may be formally compared to them. In his contribution to this volume, Leertouwer has demonstrated how the *idée directrice* of the phenomenologists comes to rule over the factual description and the explanation of religious data. This effect is still to be seen in a series of works of sociology of religion, including G. Mensching, *Soziologie der grossen Religionen* (Bonn, 1966), in which religious conceptions are not based in practical social experience, but religion on the contrary constitutes a social order of its own as a relation between the individual and the sacred.

In order to be able to apply more theories to the phenomena under examination, a general description of them is required in a preliminary working hypothesis, a generalizing theory. That short definitions of 'religion' do not offer this possibility is another reason why they are not workable. Adequate theories making it possible to examine the 'time sequence', 'evolutionary sequence' and 'causal sequence' of religious phenomena of the past will therefore be needed so that an approach can be made from various angles. We would stress that explanation in a causal sense is also involved, although we shall usually hardly rise above the level of probabilities: 'Historians deal with a universe not of absolutes but of probabilities' (Aydelotte, 1963: 175).

It has long been the fashion in comparative science of religion, especially in the branch called phenomenology, to be content with the understanding of religious structures (*Verstehen*). Since for the practitioners of the phenomenological method, G. van der Leeuw, C. J. Bleeker and others, religion is the revelation of the ultimate and supreme meaning of human existence, whose secret cannot be fathomed because it pertains to a different order, this epistemological view correlates to a theological conception. When this conception, as belonging to a different order, is admitted within the frames of reference of a discipline, there is no more need to observe epochè with regard to explanation! This does not mean that science of religion can explain the phenomenon of religion per se and in its origin; that explanation will usually be left to psychology or to philosophical and biological anthropology (cf. M. E. Spiro, 1966: 85-126). It does imply that an explanation 'for the persistence of religion' can be found with the aid of the social sciences, the behavioural sciences and psychology, especially if their theories are applied to historical phenomena.

The description of religion given by Van Baaren in the Introduction 'Science of religion as a systematic discipline', is based on the definitions formulated by Cl. Geertz and M. E. Spiro, which are determined by the problematic of social anthropology. If we are to approach history with this description, we must first of all take a closer look at the relations and tensions between the social sciences and the historical disciplines. Since Max Weber, these branches of learning have grown far apart, although in recent times a change is discernible. Within the 'humanities' there is a deep-rooted opposition to the social sciences and their practical application, which many people hold responsible for the 'dehumanization' of society. This goes back to a culturally determined grudge based on the Western individualistic tradition, in which the individual is rated more highly than the anonymous collective, the supposed object of the social sciences (cf. McGrew, 1958: 276ff.). Yet both social and historical disciplines are concerned with man and society, though from different points of view. Social sciences are more systematic, seeking the general rather than the particular, their attention is focused more on social groups than on individuals and they are more 'problem-oriented', which shows in the theories they develop. Often they pay little attention to historical aspects, so that in much research of the social sciences the time dimension is not essential. Social sciences seek for structures, and for these the factor of time is seldom essential; they work with concepts which order and give meaning to the material on the basis of a particular problematic. In a way, one might put it that social sciences create their own sources.

The historical sciences are less systematic, paying more attention to the particular than to the general and regarding historical events primarily as taking place within a certain course of time; they assume that this sequence of events has an inner ratio which will become manifest if patiently studied. These differences may be exaggerated to construct a contrast between nomothetic and idiographic sciences with fundamentally different methods. In modern research this contrast is considerably softened down, as laws have proved to be fairly general rules, while unique facts appear as elements in a pattern or a process of development, whereby they can be compared with other facts: 'uniqueness and generality are not features given in facts; they are analytical modes of appraising facts' (Cahnman-Boskoff, 1964: 4). The general and the particular must be continually weighed one against the other to arrive at explanations both in a sociological and in an historical frame of reference. The difference between social sciences and history, therefore, lies in their different emphasis with regard to the level of generalization. Regarded historically, they do not deal with different material, but they put different questions: the unique and the general supplement one another, synchronous and diachronous methods of approach to the same material are complementary. Many branches of science are becoming aware of this. Historians realize that in using terms such as 'in majority', 'elite', 'role', 'urbanization' etc. they are making quantitative and generalizing statements which the social sciences can do much to illuminate. Sociologists and cultural anthropologists realize that terms such as 'society', 'structure' and 'function' only acquire a meaning if they are used as historical categories, because it is only within a certain course of time that the entities designated by these terms have a meaning (Evans-Pritchard, 1961: 10f.). 'History is the movement by which a society reveals itself as what it is' (Louis Dumont cited by Evans-Pritchard, 1961: 12.). Thus historians such as R.E. McGrew, F. Braudel, E.H. Carr (*What is History?*, 1964), W.O. Aydelotte and others can plead for a more intensive collaboration between the two disciplines, since the kind of question posed by the social sciences may give happy inspiration to the historian, and vice versa: 'the more sociological history becomes, and the more historical sociology becomes, the better for both' (E.H. Carr, 1964: 66 cited by Lewis, 1968: xvi).

The social sciences are also beginning to pay more and more attention to history, witness the work of Cahnman-Boskoff, Lipset and Lewis, to name only a few. For scholars of totally different orientation such as Cl. Lévi-Strauss and E.E. Evans-Pritchard, there is ultimately no difference between history and cultural anthropology, as both are concerned with the study of social dynamics and social change (Lévi-Strauss: 1958, 23ff.; idem 1960: Evans-Pritchard, 1961: 10f., 18). Evans-Pritchard expresses himself most forcibly: 'history must choose between being social anthropology or being nothing' (1961: 20). In this context it is only of secondary interest that for Lévi-Strauss cultural anthropology is seeking for the 'conditions inconscientes de la vie sociale', the persistent structures of the human mind, so that for him the concept of function quite fades out and a new timelessness is apprehended.

Substantially, these identifications and attempts at rapprochement mean an endeavour to combine a diachronous and a synchronous way of approach, dropping the ethnographic present time and blending a historical and a functionalist approach: '... an interpretation on functionalist lines (of the present in terms of the present) and on historical lines (of the present in terms of the past) must somehow be combined ...' (Evans-Pritchard, 1961: 17).

In spite of the sincere intentions of many scholars working in this field, far more progress has been made with the examination of synchronous social structures than with the study of diachronous processes. 'We know a great deal about how to conceptualize in a structural-functional analysis, but we do not have the necessary concepts of process, nor the conceptual tools for significantly linking the two approaches with a general theoretical model' wrote E. Z. Vogt (1960: 18), and since then we have not got much further in the matter. As a rule the search is for all kinds of causes occasioning changes in a social structure; yet the search is *either* for economic *or* for ecological determinants, *or* for the acquiring of new cultural patterns, *or* the way of Weber is followed and the causes of change are found in the interaction of social patterns and certain values (Vogt, 1960: 18; Lipset, 1968: 37-42; Cahnman, 1964a: 116-121). Naturally this list can be supplemented with a great many variants, but the process itself remains the same. There are certain independent variables that cause changes in a socio-cultural entity. These independent variables may be sought outside a culture or inside it, they may be circumscribed or of wider effect, the process of social change always follows an analogous course (cf. Boskoff, 1964: 140-157). The problem here is that it is extremely difficult to determine which variables are independent and which are dependent. There are not really any workable theories on the 'reciprocal relations between ideas and social structures' and we are not yet able 'to specify the conditions under which aspects of social structure "produce" ideas, and vice versa' (Cahnman, 1964b: 568). Kippenberg too observes at the end of his *Forschungsbericht* that this is where the greatest problems lie for religio-social research, particularly from the historical aspect: '... man zwar verschiedene Ebenen der Gesellschaft umschreiben kann, dass aber eine Theorie der vertikalen Verbindung der Ebenen (eine Theorie der Denkformen) nur in kargen Ansätzen vorhanden ist' (Kippenberg, 1971: 81).

Of course all these theories have been useful for the better understanding and explanation of the process of social change. Each time a single variable, or even one aspect thereof, is isolated and compared with other entities. It is true that many details have to be sacrificed, but this greater level of abstraction affords a better insight in the course of the process (Lipset, 1968: 52). This method of working is applied *int. al.* in so-called structural social history and in cultural anthropology. Human society is viewed as built up of a number of groups and institutions, to several of which an individual may belong at the same time. There are all kind of relations between the various groups and institutions which may be grouped into a general model. Changes in one group, institution or sector of a culture also cause changes elsewhere, so that each time some equilibrium is broken and a new one established. This way of studying history always looks at historical data in two ways: structurally (timelessly, as it were) and evolutionally, and there is a certain tension between the two views. Variations may also be introduced with regard to the constants and variables, so that some processes may be viewed in several different constellations. The tensions are caused because structures change very little, while processes of development may be rapid. The industrial revolution in 19th century England is a clear example. The process of industrialization went on at a very fast rate, while social structures of adequate response were not yet developed. Such processes may be historically compared. The industrial revolution displays resemblances to the now beginning industrialization of the under-developed countries. The same applies to the various processes of acculturation and the process of urbanization. The latter is characterized by a greater degree of specialization in a society's division of labour, by the fact that the existing family relationships no longer determine the social order, and that there is a certain economic surplus which can be spent 'at choice'. Such processes are mutually comparable, because their course and their results may to a great extent be generalized. The religious aspects of such processes, both as regards the organizational form of the religion and an altered scale of 'needs' the religion must provide for, can be studied in these frames of reference.

A still higher degree of generalization is seen in the models or ideal types Max Weber has attempted to apply to history. Owing to this high degree of generalization, his models can only be applied to events that take place within a short period of time, since a longer period introduces too many variables which disrupt the model. Altogether Weber's œuvre becomes very important in this kind of work, since he correctly framed the problem of the relation between an individual and the totality of a culture by discerning the motivating character of a collective in the behaviour of an individual on the one hand, and on the other regarding these collectives as 'ideas' in the Kantian sense. This is the basis of his construction of ideal types. This way of regarding the matter implies 'the interpretation of holistic images in nominalistic terms. The question as to whether and to what extent Max Weber has succeeded in establishing this veritable *coincidentia oppositorum* as the cornerstone of the social sciences will provide work for social scientists for a good time to come' (Cahnman 1964a: 121). The same may be said of the work of E. Durkheim and the 'idealistic' role in it of the 'représentations collectives' (Bellah, 1964: 92 ff.). Ultimately the dominant problem in the work of both Weber and Durkheim is the connexion between conceptions and ideas and actual human behaviour, a cardinal problem for every examination of religious activities and in all religio-historical research. It is also a fundamental problem in studies of cultural anthropology, whether these distinguish between belief-, value- and action-systems or between 'patterns *for* and *of* behavior'. Whatever terminology is chosen, it always turns on the same problem, that man is not what he says he is.

All these theories and approaches, however, start from the assumption that social and cultural systems strive to maintain an equilibrium, and that social change eventuates when this equilibrium is disturbed either by external factors (cf. the theory of diffusionism, the so-called *Kulturkreislehre* and other historistic theories) or by internal factors. The course of the change is then towards the establishing of a new equilibrium. The ultimate end is the maintaining of social order and a maximum social integration. Socially loosely organized groups or a society with a minimum of correlated institutions therefore constitute a very great problem for many researchers, and are treated as marginal phenomena. It is an open question, however, whether equilibrium in this static sense is the be-all and end-all of a society. E. Z. Vogt in particular has pointed out that change is characteristic of social and cultural systems, and is not an effect of crisis to be done away with as quickly as possible. The seeming changelessness of cultures of non-literate peoples from which the models of social anthropology were developed, has helped to set up changelessness and equilibrium as indications of a maximum of social integration.

Vogt and others after him have developed theories that do indeed work with the same entities as the structural-functional models, but include the factor of change in the model. Following Weber, Durkheim, Kroeber, Kluckhohn, Geertz and others, a distinction is made between 'culture as an ordered system of meaning and symbols, in terms of which social action takes place, and social system as the pattern of social interaction itself.' (Vogt, 1960: 24). Culture is 'a patterned system', comprising a whole of values, convictions and symbols, which causes the individual to adapt to the group and reflects the group in the individual (cf. Kroeber and Kluckhohn, *Culture: A critical Review of Concepts and Definitions*; Kroeber and Talcott Parsons, 'The Concepts of Culture and social System', *American Sociological Review* 23: 582-583). In other words, culture is something like the 'meaning' informing all expressions of a society, a kind of *conscience sociale* (Durkheim), the 'super-organic' aspect of life (Cahnman). Culture is characterized by a 'logico-meaningful integration', a social system of a 'causal-functional integration' (terms taken from P. Sorokin, *Social and cultural Dynamics*, 4 Vols, N.Y. 1937). Between the two systems there is a continual tension and only rarely an equilibrium, and this tension determines the direction is which changes in the social system develop: 'The central value-orientations found in the cultural dimension of a society comprise a crucial guide-line for the directions of change' (Vogt, 1960: 25). Thus the ruling value-system does not cause the change, but provides a bed for the stream of change to flow in. Undoubtedly technological, ecological and other factors continue to play a part in causing alteration, but its effects and the way the process of change is assimilated is determined by the cultural values. Vogt has illustrated this with the ceremonial of the Navaho Indians, who in the course of their history were exposed to many different ecological, technological and religious influences. Through the central place of physical health in their cultural value-system all these influences have been selected and led in a particular direction, which can be recognized in the ceremonial.

It will be realized that the relation between individual, culture and the social system comes into view here, as in the end the changes are carried out by individuals. Is an individual entirely determined by the ruling cultural system, or has he a certain liberty of choice, a personal possibility of actualization? Without discussing all the problems of personality and culture here, it may be said that an individual is not completely determined by a cultural system, and that this involves the possibility of changes. The tension between cultural and social systems is ultimately located in man himself, who under many various influences must constantly assimilate this tension and make it bearable. 'Character embodies culture but cannot be fully described in terms of it' (Metzger, 1963: 83 ff.). The relation between the three entities may be described in the Freudian sense as id–ego–superego: an attempt to relate psychological insights, social structures and cultural values. One can also choose a 'dramaturgic' model and regard the individual primarily as playing one or more social parts (Metzger, 1963: 90 ff.) in which his personality, his social function and the cultural values meet.

I. M. Lewis also seeks the solution of the problem of 'social change' in this direction. He also points to the tension, the lack of integration between a social structure and a value-system; moreover, there is usually more than one value-system in a culture, and they are sometimes contradictory. In this situation of tension an individual chooses a part or has to fill several roles at once, serving his own ends as best he can. What is thus at stake is the 'commitment' of an individual to a social pattern, while he seeks to further his own interests to the best advantage. The function of a social system 'has meaning and utility less in its *status quo* maintenance aspects than in referring to the actual engagement and interests of people in different roles and positions' (Lewis, 1968: xxiv).

Instead of 'interests' we can say 'needs', and then wonder how all the 'needs' man feels can be satisfied. It is plain that religion serves a number of human 'needs', and we can agree with M. E. Spiro that religion has a cognitive, a substantive and an expressive function. Religion provides an answer to questions, to which no other answers can be found: 'in the absence of competitive explanations' (Spiro, 1966: 110). The questions may concern a woman's conception or the origin of the world or atmospheric phenomena such as thunder and lightning, but also suffering and death. In substance the function of religion is to conquer suffering and deficiency in all spheres of life: religion provides salvation, a copious harvest and timely rainfall. In accordance with the economic and techno-logical resources of a society, deficiencies may lie elsewhere, so that the function of religion changes as the society changes. The expressive func-tion of religion consists in the symbolic handling of many feelings and urges from the subconscious that menace the life of man. This function may comprise penitential practices, exorcisms, shamanistic séances and so on, which all serve as a vent for subconscious affections and motives.

The motives of these needs are obviously psychological, but their causes depend on the society and the opportunities it affords for the satis-faction of those needs. In Western society there is so much opportunity for active aggression, that religion can present the experience of peace as the highest ideal. Similar reasoning applies to the cognitive and the ex-pressive function, where e.g. art may fill an important role. Spiro can therefore end his exposition by observing: 'Religion, then, is to be explained in terms of society and personality' (Spiro, 1966: 122).

It will be clear that it is very difficult to work out models for more complicated societies with a wide range of subcultures. A town is a 'multicultural society' in itself, where all the subcultures often no longer have a clear structural connexion. It has been proposed, therefore, to distinguish 'culture' and 'civilization' (Cahnman, 1964b), the latter being the result of a process of urbanization. In simpler cultures it is possible to compare the belief-, value- and action-system of a single cultural sector with the respective systems of the religion, both among themselves and with one another, and to determine the relations. This applies for instance to sectors such as health, family relationships and religion, which may meet, e.g., in customs concerning food (cf. the researches of A. Jensen on the dema gods). Changes in one sector cause changes in other sectors. These changes, however, do not all proceed at the same rate, so that there is a time sequence. Thus phenomena can be synchronous or diachronous, depending on whether they are described in mathematical or historical time (Slicher van Bath, 1967: 176 ff.).

In complex cultures it is also sometimes possible to demonstrate the correlation of social and religious changes. Thus there is a clear connexion between the settling of semi-nomads in urban centres of Syria and Mesopotamia — Palmyra, Hatra, Petra —, which was accompanied by much change in social relations, and the religion which developed from various components in these towns. In this way repeated attempts will be made to distinguish a number of social sectors and institutions and to study their changes over a particular period, and then to find out the causes of these changes and the direction taken by the process, guided by the ruling values.

Finally, we must more precisely describe the importance of all this for history of religions as a historical discipline. The theoretical development of the sciences concerned with man has gradually come to a form of 'synthetic interactionism' (Voget, 1960: 953). This implies a conviction of the 'intricate interdependence of personal, social and cultural factors' in the course of that human process we are accustomed to call history. None of these is independent and immutable; only in the study of some phenomenon may the independence of one of the factors be postulated and the changes in the others studied. Thus the angle of approach to a particular problematic can be constantly changed. This is indeed desirable from a scientific point of view, for every human event is an 'interacting configuration' of the various components of reality: social, psychological, cultural, historical, functional etc. All this equally applies to history of religions, which after all studies human processes which it can only follow externally, and of which it can only observe the results. What part is due to the persons who carry out the process we cannot observe; we can only draw marginal conclusions as to that, because what we can see are only the crystallized social and cultural results of a possible psychological process. That is why the 'faith of the believers' cannot be the subject of science of religion, as it was for a historian of religion like W.B. Kristensen.

Starting from a description of religion as given by Van Baaren, we can therefore define the relation of that component of a social and cultural system which we call religion to other components, and attempt to test this historically. There is no such thing as religion 'in itself', we only meet with it in social and cultural shape. This holds even more for the historian, who can no longer observe the human conduct which shaped the forms he studies. The social sciences, which supplied the principal material for theoretical renovation in the systematical science of religion, also prove useful for history of religions in their historical aspect. They work heuristically, set up problems and provide historical work aimed at understanding man in his changing situations with a certain direction; it is 'not the formal methods of the social sciences, useful as they may be, that are of central significance, but rather their substantive findings, their intellectual concerns and their professional perspectives to open new problems ...' (Hofstadter in: Cochran-Hofstadter, 1956).

However, when interest is focused on the phenomenon of 'man', to be studied from all sides, an anthropology becomes a first requirement, for 'A human reality that can be cut like a pie, according to the "scientific" bias, can hardly further the understanding of man in nature, society and culture for very long' (Voget, 1960: 960). To nature; society and culture we may add history. An anthropology is not the final end of a science, but only an ending which may again and again become a starting-point. A good example of this is the work of Mary Douglas, *Natural Symbols. Explorations in Cosmology* (London 1970), in which social structures are correlated with the way man experiences his body, from which a fundamental symbolism is derived. Such a theory can be made historically fruitful, e.g. in studying the great dogmatic systems of Christianity and the controversies in it about the incarnation. On the other hand this theory takes us back to the beginning of all knowledge, i.e. the fundamental datum of man that he is and has a body. Here lies the possibility of religion as a human form of expression and at the same time the possibility of studying it in all its appearances, including the historical forms.

Postscriptum

After reading Leertouwer's paper in this volume the final passage of the above requires some clarification and correction. I grant that Leertouwer is right in pointing out the scientifically untenable position to which the *a priori* anthropologies of the earlier phenomenologists have led, but this does not mean that science of religion can do without an anthropology in the formal sense to make plain why man is a being who acts symbolically. Both in his and my paper the relation of ideas to social reality, or of religious conceptions to religious and non-religious behaviour is a cardinal problem, and I indeed consider that its solution can only be brought closer if it can be set forth in a general and in a formal sense what human structure this relation is rooted in. It is true that Plessner, to whom Leertouwer refers, has said 'Ein Weltall lässt sich nur glauben', but in *Die Stufen des Organischen und der Mensch* he has laid the foundation for an anthropology capable of great formalization by pointing out the ex-centric character of man's being. I think that the correlations between social structures and man's experience of his body given in Mary Douglas's *Natural Symbols* is an example of this excentricity in a social setting. I agree with Leertouwer when he says that this work does not offer an explicit anthropology, and that a model for research is something else again than faith's choice of a doctrine of man, although we can well observe in Mary Douglas herself how closely the two are linked! What I would have, however, is an anthropological model for research, which will also enable us to display the relation between committed religious anthropologies and actual human behaviour. This element in *Natural Symbols* deserves considerable emphasis.

REFERENCES

Aydelotte, W.O. (1963), 'Notes on the Problem of Historical Generalization,' pp. 145-177 in: L.G.Gottschalk (ed.), *Generalization in the Writing of History. A Report of the Committee on Historical Analysis of the Social Science Research Council.* Chicago-London, The University of Chicago Press.
— (1969), 'Quantification in History,' pp. 3-22 in: D.K.Rowney and J.Q. Graham (eds.), *Quantitative History. Selected Readings in the Quantitative Analysis of Historical Data.* Homewood, Ill., The Dorsey Press Georgetown, Ont., Irwin-Dorsey Ltd.
Baal, J. van (1971), *Symbols for Communication. An Introduction to the Anthropological Study of Religion* (Studies of Developing Countries 11). Assen, Van Gorcum & Comp.
Baird, R.D. (1968), 'Interpretative Categories and the History of Religions,' pp. 17-30 in: James S. Helfer (ed.), *On Method in the History of Religions* (History and Theory, Studies in the Philosophy of History, Beiheft 8). Wesleyan University Press.
— (1971), *Category Formation and the History of Religions* (Religion and Reason 1). The Hague-Paris, Mouton.

Bellah, R.N. (1964), 'Durkheim and History,' pp. 85-102 in W.J. Cahnman and A. Boskoff (eds.), *Sociology and History. Theory and Research* (see below).

Boskoff, A. (1964), 'Recent Theories of Social Change,' pp. 140-157 in W.J. Cahnmann and A. Boskoff (eds.), *Sociology and History. Theory and Research* (see below).

Braudel, F. (1958), 'Histoire et sciences sociales,' *Annales*, 13, pp. 725-753.

Brelich, A. (1970), 'Prolégomènes à une histoire des religions,' in H.C. Puech (ed.), *Histoire des Religions*, I. Paris, Gallimard.

Cahnman, W.J. and Boskoff, A. (eds.) (1964), *Sociology and History. Theory and Research*. Glencoe, The Free Press of Glencoe/London, Collier-Macmillan.

Cahnman, W.J. and Boskoff, A. (1964), 'Sociology and History: Reunion and Rapprochement,' pp. 1-18 in W.J. Cahnman and A. Boskoff (eds.), *Sociology and History. Theory and Research* (see above).

Cahnman, W. J. (1964a), 'Max Weber and the Methodological Controversy in the Social Sciences,' pp. 103-127 in W.J. Cahnman and A. Boskoff (eds.), *Sociology and History. Theory and Research* (see above).

Cahnman, W. J. (1964b), 'The Rise of Civilization as a Paradigm of Social Change,' pp. 537-559 in W.J. Cahnman and A. Boskoff (eds.), *Sociology and History. Theory and Research* (see above).

Cochran, Th.C. and Hofstadter, R. (1956), 'History and the Social Sciences,' pp. 347-370 in F. Stern (ed.), *The Varieties of History. From Voltaire to the Present* (Meridian Books M 37). Cleveland-New York, The World Publishing Comp.

Cochran, Th.C. (1963), 'The Historian's Use of Social Role,' pp. 103-110 in: Gottschalk (ed.), *Generalization in the Writing of History. A Report of the Committee on Historical Analysis of the Social Science Research Council*. Chicago-London, The University of Chicago Press.

Douglas, Mary (1970), *Natural Symbols. Explorations in Cosmology*. London, Routledge & Kegan Paul.

Evans-Pritchard, E.E. (1961), *Anthropology and History*. Manchester, Manchester University Press.

Finley, M.I. (1963), 'Generalizations in Ancient History,' pp. 19-35 in: L.G.Gottschalk (ed.), *Generalization in the Writing of History. A Report of the Committee on Historical Analysis of the Social Science Research Council*. Chicago-London, The University of Chicago Press.

Historia Religionum (1969). Vol. I: Religions of the past. Ed. by C.J.Bleeker and G.Widengren. Leiden, E.J.Brill.

Kippenberg, H.G. (1971), 'Wege zu einer historischen Religionssoziologie. Ein Literaturbericht,' pp. 54-82 in: *Verkündigung und Forschung. Religionen-*

Mission-Ökumene (Beihefte zu 'Evangelische Theologie' 2/1971). München, Kaiser Verlag.

Lévi-Strauss, Cl. (1958), 'Introduction. Histoire et ethnologie,' pp. 3-33 in: *Anthropologie structurale*. Paris, Librairie Plon.

— (1960), 'L'anthropologie structurale devant l'histoire,' *Annales*, 15, pp. 625-637.

Lewis, I.M. (1968), 'Introduction' in I.M. Lewis, *History and Social Anthropology* (A.S.A. Monographs 7). London-New York, Tavistock Publications.

Lipset, S.M. (1968), 'History and Sociology: Some Methodological Considerations', pp. 20-58 in: S.M. Lipset and R. Hofstadter (eds.), *Sociology and History: Methods*. New York-London: Basic Books, I.MC, Publications.

McGrew, R.E. (1958), 'History and the Social Sciences,' *The Antioch Review*, 18, pp. 276-289.

Metzger, W.P. (1963), 'Generalizations about National Character: An Analytical Essay,' pp. 77-102 in: L.G.Gottschalk (ed.), *Generalization in the Writing of History. A Report of the Committee on Historical Analysis of the Social Science Research Council*, Chicago-London, The University of Chicago Press.

Rudolph, K. (1971), 'Das Problem einer Entwicklung in der Religionsgeschichte,' *Kairos*, XIII, pp. 95-118.

Slicher van Bath, B.H. (1967), *Theorie en praktijk in de economische en sociale geschiedenis* (Afdeling Agrarische Geschiedenis Landbouwhogeschool Wageningen, Bijdragen 14), pp. 105-228.

Smith, M. (1968), 'Historical Method in the Study of Religion,' pp. 8-16 in: J.S. Helfer (ed.), *On Method in the History of Religions* (History and Theory, Studies in the Philosophy of History, Beiheft 8). Wesleyan University Press.

Spiro, M.E. (1966), 'Religion: Problems of Definition and Explanation,' pp. 85-126 in M. Banton (ed.), *Anthropological Approaches to the Study of Religion*. London, Tavistock Publications.

Starr, Ch.G. (1963) 'Reflections upon the Problem of Generalization,' pp. 3-18 in: L. Gottschalk (ed.), *Generalization in the Writing of History. A. Report of the Committee on Historical Analysis of the Social Science Research Council*. Chicago-London, The University of Chicago Press.

Voget, F.W. (1960), 'Man and Culture: An Essay in Changing Anthropological Interpretation,' *American Anthropologist*, 62, pp. 943-965.

Vogt, E.Z. (1960), 'On the Concepts of Structure and Process in Cultural Anthropology,' *American Anthropologist*, 62, pp. 18-33.

Yinger, J.M. (1970), *The Scientific Study of Religion*. London-New York, The Macmillan Company.

Inquiry into Religious Behaviour
A Theoretical Reconnaissance

PHENOMENOLOGISTS ON RELIGIOUS BEHAVIOUR

Naturally, one would say, religious behaviour is an important subject of research for the science of religion. Yet a quick look through the systematic hand-books of science of religion tends to show the reverse: it is only the exceptional work which acknowledges behaviour as an independent category of phenomena. A systematic methodology of research into religious behaviour has not yet been set up; the formation of theories in the behavioural sciences in a more general sense has not yet influenced discussion in the science of religion, or barely so, and by no means led to a religious ethology. As a rule religious actions are described and interpreted as no more than illustrations of religious ideas or convictions.

Two examples may illustrate this. G. van der Leeuw (1956: 382 ff.) sees religious behaviour, in which he distinguishes 'external' and 'internal' action, as a form of interaction between man and the world. With Heidegger, he characterizes this interaction as *Sorge*. The specific behavioural form of religion is the observance: *Benehmen* becomes *Begehen*. For in religion concern becomes fear; out of this fear the ritual is born as a special form of behaviour. This approach to religious behaviour in terms of existentialist philosophy has far-reaching consequences: 1) the scale of possible motives for ritual action is thereby reduced to a single one — a 'fear' which is not capable of empirical verification. This reduction is consistent with Van der Leeuw's dynamistic thinking (cf. Van Baaren, 1964: 103 ff.), but in conflict with the many forms of 'internal action' he manages to enumerate (1956: 522 ff.) and more importantly, it is no longer credible when we leave the field of contemplative existentialist philosophy for the reality of ritual acts, when not only fear but also many other motives such as prestige, community feeling or sexual urge are seen to play an important part. 2) In this view religious behaviour is restricted to the category of ritual action. The large group of phenomena which Van Baaren (1973: 393 ff.) calls 'the second form of religious action' is neglected here. Even without fully subscribing to Van Baaren's descriptions — I shall return to some objections — it must be said that the onesidedness of Van der Leeuw's outlook threatens to blind science of religion to the complicated relations subsisting between religion and other cultural functions which count particularly for behaviour. 3) Thus for Van der Leeuw religious behaviour — ritual, in his conception — becomes both in the historical and in the structural sense the model of all behaviour: culture is no other than secularized cult. This theory regards religion as the nucleus of any given culture, neglecting the interdependence of cultural functions and isolating the religious phenomena; at best, it is indeed 'a return in a real sense to Medievalism', as one of its most recent defenders has called it. (Miller, 1964: 93).

Far less than Van der Leeuw does Widengren feel the need of starting from a philosophical anthropological concept. According to him, science of religion may confine itself to the classification of religious phenomena. (Widengren, 1969: 1) Yet he who classifies must indicate what structures he has discovered in the various configurations of phenomena, or at least what structures he wishes to impose upon these phenomena, since it is from this ordering that he takes his criteria of classification. Widengren tells us nothing of this, however. Hence an enumeration he gives of forms of religious behaviour gives an impression of arbitrariness. When in the same context he reflects on the essence of ritual (1969: 209 ff.), he again discusses various more or less important characteristics of ritual acts, but gives no definition at all.

Both Van der Leeuw and Widengren, however different their approach, are phenomenologists. The phenomenological method prevents both from doing justice to religious behaviour as a comparatively independent category of phenomena.

We must enter more fully into this handicap of the phenomenologist in studying religious behaviour. For it is still phenomenology of religion, at least on the continent of Europe, which is accounted *the* method of systematic science of religion, in spite of the fact that precisely problems of method are little attended to by phenomenologists. Van Baaren's remonstrance against the faults in phenomenology of religion (1973:9 ff.) need not be repeated here. I am concerned to show what consequences the use of phenomenology as a method has for the study of religious behaviour.

Recently A. Brelich (1970: XVII ff.) once set forth the positive aspects of the phenomenological approach to religions. In his opinion, and I agree with him on this point, its great merit lies in the consistent treat-ment of the material from one well-chosen central idea, developed from the phenomena according to uniform principles. As long as this *idée directrice* is made sufficiently explicit, and especially as long as it is handled in a sufficiently formal fashion, one need not deny that phe-nomenology of religion has the merits Brelich ascribes to it.

Unfortunately, however, the *idée directrice* of the phenomenologists, whether it be power, the sacred or the conception of god, nearly always proves to be not only a formal principle of order, but also to rule over the description and explanation of the religious phenomena with regard to their content. In explanation, which as Van Baaren justly remarks, most phenomenologists are loth to enter into, this compulsive role of the *idée directrice* appears most clearly, because the idea is often formulated in such a way that any scientific explanation is excluded a priori. Concepts such as 'the power' and 'the sacred' are in fact mystifications and therefore not suitable for the explanation of empiric data. Moreover they stand in the way of other explanations: when cultural anthropologists and other sociological researchers try to elucidate religious data by establishing what asymmetrical human relationships they reflect, and precisely who or what is inviolable (sacred), i.e. when they attempt to find an empirical foundation for the power and the sacred, they are only too often re-proached from the phenomenological side with being reductionists. This reproach is ridiculous: every science reduces reality, and phenom-enology does so too. Indeed, phenomenology itself is often to be accused of reducing after the fashion of Morgenstern's guineafowl (Perlhuhn) (1952: 199): *Es zählt, von Wissendrang gejückt, (die es sowohl wie uns entzückt:) die Anzahl seiner Perlen.* The power and the sacred are such imaginary pearls; they contribute as little to the knowledge of religion as the assiduously counting fowl does to ornithology.

In methodological terms the above may be summarized as follows: concepts such as power and the sacred require to function within a deductive explana-tory model. Such a model attempts to set forth from what causes and under what necessary conditions certain spatially and temporally specified events may occur. These constitute the *explananda* of the model; the central idea (the power, the sacred) has a part in the *explanans*. Now it is very difficult to define the exact role of these concepts; it is possible, however, to make up methodical rules to which the explanans must in any case conform. Following C. G. Hempel (1965: 334-496), the methodologist Karl-Dieter Opp (1970: 29 ff.) posits that the explanans must at any rate comply with the following requirements: it must contain at least one statement embodying an empirical norm or rule (R) and at least one statement concerning the initial necessary conditions (C) of the explanandum; furthermore explanans and explanandum must be true.

Let us take as an example the explanation Van der Leeuw (1956: 213 ff.) gives of a form of behaviour: circumcision. In a simplified form this runs:

R(ule):   When mutilation is practised in a ritual, then the rite is intended to express a symbolic death and resurrection.
C(ondition): Circumcision comprises mutilation.
E(xplanandum): Circumcision is a symbolic death and resurrection.

This reasoning supplies a partial explanation of the phenomenon which answers to the conditions of the model and, partly because of that, is satisfactory. The concept of power does not come into it at all; yet Van der Leeuw continues: 'Sie (circumcision) ist nur einer der vielerlei Riten, die Machtzufuhr oder -erneuerung bezwecken' (1956: 213). This addition, which in terms of the explanatory model is superfluous and arbitrary, has nothing to do with the phenomenon of circumcision, but all the more with the easy definition of the subject of phenomenology that we find in the same chapter (Van der Leeuw, 1956: 208): 'Die Phänomenologie beschreibt, wie der Mensch sich zur Macht verhält.' The artless reader thinks that phenomenology of religion is here ... reduced to political sociology. This proves not to be the intention at all, for further on (1956: 303) it is just the social sciences which are reproached with allowing the religious to be entirely subsumed in the social category.

That this reduction is most useful for arriving at a meaningful explanation of religious behaviour, is shown by V. Turner in his study of circumcision among the Ndembu (Zambia) (Turner, 1967: 151 ff.). During his field work he had collected two groups of data, one concerning the social system of the Ndembu and the other concerning details of ritual and their interpretation, and also what he calls 'items of secular behavior' directly connected with the observance and maintenance of the complex of rites. Acting on the hypothesis that under the surface there must be many links between the two, he sought a model of interpretation capable of bringing to light the correlations. He found this model in the so-called 'field theory' of Kurt Lewin (1949, cf. Mey, 1972). The principal characteristic of this theory is that the frontier between an individual organism and its environment is regarded as fluid and diffuse, meaning that persons and groups operate in an 'organism-environment field'; the phenomena observed in this field are considered as appertaining *to the field*, they are 'field properties'.

As far as I know, Turner is the first cultural anthropologist to apply Lewin's originally psychological theory to the problem discussed here: the relations between religious and social phenomena. His results are impressive: by reducing the cultural and religious data to elements in a cultural field, both kinds of data show to full advantage and relations appear between them which had remained hidden up till now, both from science of religion and from the socio-logical approach based on structural or functional analysis. In the present context I cannot attempt even to give an inventory of Turner's harvest from his research into the rites of circumcision. I will only mention a single point: the part played by the concept of 'power' for Turner as contrasted with Van der Leeuw's use of the term.

One of Turner's informants stressed to him that 'Mukanda (the ritual of circumcision, LL) is to cure a novice, that he may be strong, that he may catch power' (Turner, 1967: 153). This information seems to confirm Van der Leeuw's view that circumcision aims at *Machtzufuhr oder -erneuerung*. Unlike Van der Leeuw, however, Turner does not link this statement with a mys-terious concept of 'power' beyond all verification, but with the myths relating the origin of circumcision and with the processes taking place between people in and around the ritual. His application of the field theory enables him to define the concept of power very exactly in operational terms. Following Lewin, he speaks of a 'power-field'. 'Power' means for him the possibility residing in an individual or a group to exercise power, power of a definite extent, over another individual or another group. Turner then shows how the decision to celebrate the ritual of circumcision turns the 'power-field' into a field of forces, and he is able to indicate quite exactly what movements are thus engendered among the various elements in the field. (1967: 267ff.) It is striking that the role of the religious elements can now be described with a clarity rarely equalled, instead of sinking down behind the social elements in a superficial reductionism. What a poor figure phenomenological analysis makes by comparison!

Yet it is not only upon the level of the explanation of behaviour but also in its description that science of religion handicaps itself by operating with concepts such as 'power' and 'the sacred'. The danger here lies in limitation of the outlook of the researcher, through his inclination to use these concepts as indications of 'the essence' of religion; they then tend to play a normative dogmatic role in the ordering and selection of data. Texts seem to submit more easily to such dogmatic dictation than human behaviour. This is not only illustrated by the history of Christian theology, but also by Wagenvoort's treatment of the textual material of Roman religion and by Van der Leeeuw's handling of the Old Testament texts (Wagenvoort, 1941, and Van der Leeuw, 1956), to name only two famous examples.

There may be a connexion with the fact that phenomenologists have traditionally tended to concentrate upon the doctrine of the religion studied, and have devoted little systematic thought to the complex correlations between the *Gedankengut* of a religion on the one hand and the factual behaviour of the believers on the other. When the behavioural aspects are not entirely disregarded, they only take second rank and are really no more than illustrations of the doctrine, or even of the *idée directrice* chosen as point of departure and as nucleus.

This treatment of behaviour as the illustration of an idea or a complex of ideas is a most undesirable simplification of reality. Human actions, including those we are accustomed to call 'religious acts', form part of a *pattern* of behaviour. This will be more fully discussed below, but without anticipating we may suppose that, apart from biological determinants, this pattern — in so far as it is accessible to scientific research — is not fortuitous and unique, but acquired by learning and dependent on initial necessary conditions in the social and cultural field. The phenomenological way of treating religious behaviour as a kind of depiction of an idea would suggest a direct and unilateral dependence. Most socio-cultural stimuli can awaken more than one reaction, while conversely an action usually responds to more than one motivating stimulus. It is an artifice, therefore, to couple a single religious motif and a single act which is regarded as religious; this threatens to reduce religious behaviour to a series of religiously conditioned reflexes, besides isolating it from its socio-cultural milieu. A description of religious behaviour according to its ideal type such as phenomenology wishes to give, is therefore always in danger of reverting to its opposite, so that *homo religiosus* coincides with a religious variant of the dogs of Pavlov. I will not deny that such a conditioned form of religious behaviour may exist in fact, but that is no justification for elevating such an exception to the position of model.

In particular the study of the religions of non-literate peoples supplies alarming examples of caricatures resulting from a wrongly chosen and dogmatically handled set of theoretical concepts. (cf. Van Baaren, 1964, passim) I will only name two complexes of problems connected with religious behaviour, where the phenomenology of power has played a really disastrous part: the connection between myth and rite and the question of the motivation of religious action. On the basis of the schema 'predone-redone', whereby the repetition of the rite is regarded as an attempt to re-activate the forces permanently stored in the myth, the rite has been conceived as an automatic repetition *ex opere operato*. As especially Ad. E. Jensen has shown, behaviour thereby loses its historical dimension, since the interpretation of a ritual by a particular group of interested persons in a usually late phase of historical development, is without further consideration regarded as the key to understanding of the phenomenon in itself. (Jensen, 1951; cf. Leertouwer, 1967).

For the second example I refer to the work of P. Radin (1951, 1957). His research shows what mistakes have been made in the interpretation of religious behaviour because the great differences in degree of commitment among participants in the same religious culture, as well as the variations in behaviour of various groups and individuals owing to different psychological motivation have been disregarded or levelled down in a tight theoretical schema. We find that traditional phenomenology's description of religious behaviour in its ideal type means an idealization of religion; the objections to this are not only scientific but also social.

In summarizing the objections to the way phenomenology of religion deals with behaviour I would turn to the final remarks of Drijvers in his contribution to the present volume. He there points out the necessity of an anthropological concept as the terminal point of research in science of religion, a terminal point which at any moment can again become a starting-point. I cannot entirely subscribe to this opinion. In the foregoing the objections to the phenomenological treatment of religious behaviour were concentrated upon its *idées directrices*, in so far as these contained an explicit or implicit anthropology by which the choice and interpretation of the data was determined beforehand. It is true that by referring to the work of Mary Douglas, Drijvers in part allays our fear that he might wish to continue the aprioristic anthropology of earlier phenomenologists — yet only in part. For in my opinion Mary Douglas's *Natural Symbols* does not contain an explicit anthropology, at least not in the sense of a doctrine of man that could be the starting-point and the terminal point of thought in the science of religion. At most, she supplies material for it, just as her colleagues Codrington and Preuss did for the phenomenologist Van der Leeuw. On the analogy of Plessner's pronouncement 'Ein Weltall läszt sich nur glauben', I think that also 'an anthropology' is a matter of faith: the choice of a model for research is something entirely different from faith's choice of a doctrine of man. That the two are often connected I will not deny, but it seems to me that science of religion, which is still laboriously emancipating itself from the nursery of theology, does well to maintain a strict distinction here. In any case an anthropological concept used as starting-point of a theory in science of religion will need to be capable of a high degree of formalization if the a prioris of the past are to be avoided. In the following I will try to set up a few criteria for this.

RELIGION AND BEHAVIOUR

In Van Baaren's contribution to this book (1973: 39) we find an attempt at defining what religious behaviour really is. With him also, of course, the definition depends on what he wishes to understand by religion. I must therefore make a few remarks about Van Baaren's description of religion before discussing his conception of religious behaviour.

Van Baaren's description builds on the definitions he quotes by Geertz and Spiro (Geertz, 1966; Spiro, 1966). Yet there is an essential difference between his words and the two American definitions, and this difference seems very important for the formulation of the concept 'religious behaviour'. The difference appears right at the beginning, where Van Baaren describes religion as 'a complex of notions which as a rule form a more or less connected system'.

This choice of words evidences a certain reserve towards the concept 'cultural system' used by both Geertz and Spiro. Leaving this aside, my concern is with the characterization of religion as a complex of *notions*. Geertz speaks of a system of symbols, Spiro of an institution consisting of interaction between human and superhuman beings. The first description is of a *culturological*, the second of a more *sociological* kind. Van Baaren's preference for the term 'notions' is that of the *phenomenologist*, interested especially in the cognitive function of religion.

The term 'notions', however, is used by Van Baaren on various levels, without its becoming quite clear what the correlations are between these levels. First of all there is the general reference to a complex of notions, among which those concerning superior beings and/or powers are of particular importance. Through becoming part of human faith, this category of notions exercises a certain influence upon human existence. This influence then becomes apparent *int. al.* in behaviour and actions, but also in new notions. Thus there is a kind of hierarchy of notions. (cf. Fig. 1) Here we must, I think, speak

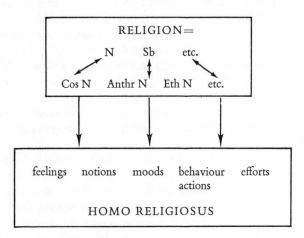

Fig. 1   Religion according to Van Baaren

N = Notion   Anthr = Anthropological
Sb = Superior beings   Cos   = Cosmological
                           Eth   = Ethical

of 'some muddles in the models' (cf. Schneider, 1965). The correlation between *N Sb*, etc. and *Cos N Anthr N Eth N*, etc. is reasonably clear, especially in view of Van Baaren's appreciation of Spiro's definition (1973: 36): in the structure of the 'complex' religion *N Sb* are a kind of centres; the description suggests that *Cos ... Eth N*, etc. are *logically* dependent on *N Sb*, etc. Geertz does not enter into the problem of dependence; for his model it is sufficient to establish that the 'system of symbols' influences people through generating 'conceptions of a general order of existence': their content might coincide with Van Baaren's *N Sb + Cos N ... Eth N*, etc. (cf. Geertz, 1966: 4). In Spiro's model, on the other hand, the structurally dominant position of *N Sb* must be stressed, as this position is an initial necessary condition for the validity of the whole definition: no interaction without $N\ Sb$ (cf. Spiro, 1966: 97). By combining the models of these two Van Baaren has introduced a third group of notions which, he says, are divided into a cultic and a socio-ethical group. He also seems to follow Spiro where the latter distinguishes two types of activity: 1) activities which, the faithful assume, reflect the value system of the superhuman beings (that would be Van Baaren's socio-ethical aspect) and 2) activities which, the faithful assume, can influence the superhuman beings to satisfy human needs. (Van Baaren's cultic ritual notions).

It seems to me that Van Baaren's third group of notions coincides with his second group, so that it only confuses the model and would be better left out. For if we call the socio-ethical notions $Se\ N$ and the cultic ritual ones $Cr\ N$, then we see in Van Baaren's model: $Se\ N + Cr\ N = Cos\ N \dots Eth\ N$.

Yet if we eliminate the third group in this fashion, a new problem arises. In the enumeration Van Baaren gives of the elements of the world of religious experience (feelings etc. ending with efforts) notions cannot be left out, since they form an integral part of religious life. On the other hand the series $Cos\ N \dots Eth\ N$ cannot be scrapped either, for these notions belong to the *Erscheinungswelt der Religion*.

This impasse must, I think, lead to the conclusion that the description as a whole has been insufficiently thought out. The culturological and the sociological approach may very well be combined, but the combination cannot be described in phenomenological terms. As soon as one abstracts from the socio-cultural field of which 'religion' is a sector, one can say that religion is a complex of notions; if with Van Baaren one takes religion to be a part of culture, or even a function of it, the description no longer holds because it does not include religious behaviour and religious values. Yet if one forcibly introduces behaviour and values into the complex of notions, the consequences are unacceptable as was already shown above, for then the pattern of behaviour is made directly dependent on the system of notions, and thus isolated from the socio-cultural field where it is active.

This mistake in method has notable consequences when such theoretical concepts are adduced in the study of historical problems. (cf. Drijvers, 1973: 10ff.) If changes in religious behaviour are studied over a certain length of time, then this conception only allows of their explanation if changes of notion can be demonstrated at the same time; strictly speaking these two changes would also need to be of comparable compass, and moreover the place taken in the whole pattern of behaviour by the change in question would require to be demonstrably analogous with the place of the corresponding change in the complex of notions. It need hardly be argued that such will very rarely be the case. Changes in behaviour such as for instance the 'Vailala-madness' in Australian New Guinea described by Worsley and others (cf. Worsley, 1957) would even become entirely inexplicable, for the abrupt change in behaviour of the Papuans was motivated more by the international monetary crisis of 1929 than by their own religious ideas; the change in ideas came afterwards: in this case it was a function of changing behaviour and not the other way round.

For this reason I consider Spiro's description more serviceable for the theory of religious behaviour than Van Baaren's, whose objection that it is rather vague I do not share. It seems to me that Spiro gives the exact crux of the matter when people behave according to a pattern that we call religious: interaction between men and the superhuman beings postulated by them, while this interaction is of an institutional nature. To this institutional character also belongs a complex of notions, part of which (the $N\ Sb$) form the initial necessary conditions for the arising of this interaction, while part arise as functions of the interaction. The interaction itself one might call the behavioural aspect of what Geertz calls the 'system of symbols'.

The analysis given above of Van Baaren's description of religion shows that he really divides all notions except those connected with superior beings into two categories: $Se\ N$ and $Cr\ N$. His treatment of religious behaviour follows the same classification: $Se\ N : Cr\ N = Se\ B : Cr\ B$ (B = behaviour). $Cr\ B$ he calls symbolic behaviour; $Se\ B$ is not given a separate name; we will just call this category non-symbolic behaviour. Behaviour may be called symbolic, when it 'can only be regarded as meaningful and fit to the purpose *within* the framework of a religion' (Van Baaren, *l.c.*); it is not symbolic if it is also regarded as meaningful and fit to the purpose outside the framework of religion, and so regarded after the same manner as within it.

Here Van Baaren seems to be following the criteria of the anthropologist S. F. Nadel. (Nadel, 1951: 28 ff., cf. Tennekes, 1971: 80 ff.) To qualify as 'behaviour', Nadel demands that actions should answer to the following three requirements: 1) the behaviour must to some extent be *standardized* (be recurrent, regular, coherent and predictable). This is probably what Van Baaren means when he uses the term 'meaningful'. Unique, unpredictable, irregular and incoherent actions can quite well be meaningful in metaphysical terms, but not in terms of cultural science. 2) Only those forms of behaviour are to be considered by the anthropologist which are *fit to a purpose* ('can be expressed in terms of a task'). 3) The behaviour must be *social* in an empirical sense: 'behavior of man in the group'. Van Baaren does not name this requirement, but it is implicit in this conception of religion as a part of culture.

Having regard to Spiro's view that a cultural system may be divided into three sub-systems: the *belief* system, the *value* system and the *action* system (Spiro, 1964: 102ff.), we may formulate Van Baaren's view as follows: religious behaviour is to be called symbolic when the symbolic elements of the belief system ($N\,Sb + Cos\,N \ldots Eth\,N$) form initial necessary conditions for the explanation of that behaviour.

As an example I shall take Christian Holy Communion according to the Protestant rite (the ritual variants among the various denominations may be disregarded here). The explanation of this ritual will have to make use of data that are not derived from the cultural system 'religion', but from other systems or parts thereof: in this case the most important of these is the system 'food'. These elements, like the corresponding ones of the system 'religion', require to be placed in a historical context, because the choice of food and drink, and also its handling during the ritual, are derived from a culture other than that in which the ritual chiefly functions at the moment. It then appears that these non-religious elements play an important part in explaining the ritual; the symbolic elements from the belief system of religion are however decisive as initial necessary conditions (cf. Fig. 2).

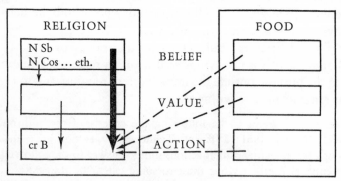

Fig. 2.   *Determinants of behaviour in a ritual action*
N   = notions   Anthr = anthropological
cr B = cultic ritual behaviour   Cos   = cosmological
Sb   = superior beings   Eth   = ethical
(only those relations have been marked which are important for cultic ritual behaviour)

Such a schema only holds for an element of Cr B, not for Se B. A believer's choice for a Christian-democrat party, for instance, *may* be connected with his views regarding N Sb + Cos N ... Eth N, but these views can never form the initial necessary conditions for the explanation of his behaviour as a voter.

This translation of Van Baaren's views into methodological terms can eliminate a misunderstanding to which his formulation might lead. For when he names 'natural sciences and technics, psychology or social sciences' as other departments of culture besides religion, in which Cr B cannot, but Se B may perhaps be regarded as meaningful and fit to the purpose in the same way as it is so regarded in the department of religion, then he is silently introducing a tertium comparationis which I do not think is in place here. (cf. Horton, 1968) The typical characteristic of the cultural system 'science' is, that the essence of its belief and value system is to place the belief and value system of other departments of culture in a position of relativity. (cf. Elias, 1970: 110ff.) In the West at any rate, this department thus takes up an exceptional position.

It is not a matter of chance that only very few 'actors' within the action system of science succeed in making their behaviour as participants in a culture entirely congruous with the conceptions and values of science; fortunately indeed, for in all other departments of culture they would become complete outsiders! The conflict between faith and science which Van Baaren's choice of examples introduces into the context of the problem of 'religious behaviour', deserves a separate discussion and is best left out of account here.

With this restriction, we can accept Van Baaren's classification as a useful distinction. It is of importance especially because it directs the attention of science of religion upon non-symbolic behaviour as an expression of religion, a field in which far too little research has so far been done by our discipline. As remarked before, it was either neglected, or the mistaken theoretical presupposition that it was a secularized form of ritual behaviour — Van der Leeuw's theory — was held to suffice. The dismissal of this romantic construction, however, still leaves us with the problem how these two categories of behaviour are to be related. Nor does Van Baaren supply an answer. One may suppose, though, that he too makes Se B dependent in a sense upon Cr B. For if our hypothesis that in Van Baaren's description $Se\ N : Cr\ N = Se\ B : Cr\ B$, wherein

$Se\ N + Cr\ N$ coincides with $Cos\ N \dots Eth\ N$ and as such is dependent upon $N\ Sb$ is right, then this logical dependence of notion one upon the other would also imply a certain dependence of $Se\ B$ upon $Cr\ B$. In the model of Geertz this is indeed the case, and that in a psychological sense. Ritual behaviour clothes conceptions of a general order of existence with such a unique quality of truth that they can also determine, or rather help to determine, behaviour outside the ritual. This 'higher value', however, is not constant: it may be reduced to zero if cultic ritual behaviour no longer manages to convey an 'aura of factuality' upon this unique quality of truth of the religious conceptions. Hence Geertz has to apply criteria of effectivity to ritual behaviour in its relation with the belief system, so that he speaks of ritual success and ritual failure. (Geertz, 1958: 421 ff.; 1960) To correct a too one-sided use of Van Baaren's description with its primacy of notions over actions, the view of Geertz is useful; yet it should not be forgotten that it is of a psychological nature and derives from a different problematic: he is not treating the problem of the structure of religion, but the problem of the effectivity of religious behaviour, while religion is seen as a process of learning undergone with more or less success by individuals and groups.

In this context we must finally inquire after the relative range of the two kinds of religious behaviour. A religion such as Christianity, for instance, has had several periods in its history when the two were in conflict. At the time of the breaking of images in the Netherlands during the Reformation, the two forms were entirely out of equilibrium. We have seen that, apart from a certain tendency to make $Se\ B$ dependent on $Cr\ B$, Van Baaren does not enter into this question. Spiro does, however, and so we will give a short description of his views. It is of interest that the problem leads him to define symbolism very differently from Van Baaren.

Spiro's description of the two kinds of behaviour we have already discussed and compared with that of Van Baaren (cf. p. 87 ff.). The two kinds may overlap, but never coincide ('are never coterminous', Spiro 1966: 96). Where they overlap, Spiro says, the behaviour will be of a strongly symbolic character. Otherwise than Van Baaren, therefore, Spiro does not reserve the term symbolic for one of the two types of activity, but only for the sphere where they overlap. By 'symbolic' behaviour Spiro understands a system of activities whose meaning, 'cross-culturally viewed, is obscure and/or arbitrary; and whose efficacy, scientifically viewed, is not susceptible of ordinary scientific "proof". These symbolic, but definitely instrumental, activities constitute, of course, a *ritual*, or symbolic *action system*.' (Spiro, *l.c.*)

These two scholars reserve the term 'symbolic' for ritual actions, but their criteria for giving this name to a particular form of activity are different. Spiro is of opinion that an action may only be called symbolic if its meaning, when compared with other cultures and when measured by the standards of western science, appears obscure or arbitrary. These criteria seem inadmissible to me. I do not see why we need have recourse to intercultural comparison to be able to denote the symbolic character of an action; this may very well be done in the framework of a single culture, by comparison with other parts of that culture, as Van Baaren would do. The second criterion, that of scientific effectivity, does not seem applicable either; I would refer to what was remarked above with regard to Van Baaren's incidental appeal to the natural sciences etc. (cf. p. 91). For that matter, very little of Spiro's two types of activity will survive cross-cultural comparison and application of the norma of scientific efficacy: neither the value system of superhuman beings nor the power ascribed to them of satisfying human needs, regarded as meaningful motivation of behaviour, can pass that test!

For the present we shall have to be content to observe that the relationship between cultic ritual behaviour and 'non-symbolic' behaviour is still in many respects *terra incognita*. Van Baaren's distinction offers a good startingpoint for science of religion to enter upon this field. I imagine that the necessity of profiting here by the theories formulated by the behavioural sciences will to some extent have become evident from the foregoing. As regards the role of symbols in a (religious) pattern of behaviour, it is in order here to remind him who would undertake research in this matter of the warning of Duncan, who has written an excellent book on 'symbolic action': 'As powerful as religious belief may be in organizing social relationships, it is but *one* kind of belief.' (Duncan, 1969: 279).

BEHAVIOURAL STUDIES IN SCIENCE OF RELIGION

Duncan's warning, however salutary, may have a discouraging effect. If research into religious behaviour must *also* take account of the many other forms of belief that beside and interwoven with religion in the stricter sense operate in the socio-cultural field and influence human behaviour, then does not the picture become far too complicated? We can no longer make use of the theological distinction between true and pseudo-religion; we see a chasm between Schleiermacher's religion with its *eigene Provinz im Gemüthe* and Van Baaren's 'religion as a part of culture', that the slender means of science of religion and its students are insufficient to bridge over. What is left, moreover, of the independence and integrity of science of religion (the expression is Kurt Rudolph's) if in order to do justice to a part of its subject — religious behaviour — it is forced to infiltrate so deeply in the field of social sciences?

Whoever, like the present author, realizes what a small step was taken in the foregoing in the direction of the behavioural sciences, and how often we put up with shocking simplifications, cannot avoid this question. Nor can I give a satisfactory answer. What I can say is, that this task cannot be left to others with anything like a tranquil conscience. The theoretical progress in the social sciences with regard to religion cannot be called impressive, as Van Baal (1971: VII) recently reminded us. The distance between those who have empirical information about religion and those who plan sociological theories is large, and it is too large. Science of religion is thereby offered, if not a legitimation, at any rate a most valid excuse for venturing upon the field.

In my opinion this will demand a lot of theoretical work. Historians of religion are historians or philologists by training, and therefore they often have a traditionally determined dislike for theorizing. Yet now that both the historical and the linguistic discipline are changing upon this point, it will be necessary to arrive at something like a theoretical science of religion. Not indeed to design another 'theory of religion', but to construct partial models, making the results of the various disciplines which are implicitly or explicitly concerned with religion available for useful mutual discussion.

Among suitable subjects for such work, one of the first is religious behaviour, too long neglected as it has been. We will not overestimate the share of science of religion in its traditional form. As regard behaviour, this discipline has for the present more to learn than to teach. On the other hand there is no reason to underestimate its possibilities. It may be seen from the above that religious conceptions may play a decisive part in behaviour. These conceptions are the traditional subject of science of religion. It would be a good step forward if in studying religious conceptions serious account was taken of their relation to behaviour. In a study of the Windigo psychosis, a mental illness among North American Indians which rests on religious motifs, Morton I. Teicher (1960: 113) has shown that 'the profound impact of belief on behavior has all the quality of a determining force'. There is no reason to limit the validity of this pronouncement to North America or to psychotic behaviour, since Teicher's research also shows that this impact not only holds good for these directly concerned, but also for other participants in the same culture. That this relation has not always been appreciated at its full value in the West, has something to do with Christianity, a religion in which the faithful are accustomed to take the truths served up to them with a good many more pinches of salt than the theologians had meant. Connected with this is the fact that science of religion has contributed considerably to the *idealization* of religion and religious behaviour. If it is to avoid this fault in the future, then it must once again turn for guidance to cultural anthropology. For this discipline makes a consistent methodical distinction between patterns of behaviour as complexes of behavioural *norms* on the one hand, and as complexes of factual behaviour on the other. In the terms of Clyde Kluckhohn (1954: 924) 'Patterns *for* and *of* behavior' (cf. Kroeber-Kluckhohn, 1963: 341; Nadel 1951: 78; Tennekes, 1971: 80ff.). The pattern for behaviour is only *one* of the determinants influencing the pattern of behaviour. Science of religion will probably have to leave the factual pattern of behaviour largely to the social sciences, if only because it has not mastered the quantitative methods necessary for the study of factual behaviour (cf. Argyle, 1958: 11-20). It can, however, take note of the results and make use of them in working out the normative pattern of religious behaviour, and that is what it will have to do. For now that science of religion is more and more required to explain religious behaviour to believers and unbelievers, the idealization of religious behaviour becomes a social danger. That is another matter, however; even though science of religion itself forms part of the cultural system 'religion', there is no need for it simply to take over the faults of that system.

NOTE

Prof. Van Baaren's article was written after lengthy discussion in the Groningen Working Group, and forms in part the outcome of those discussions, in which the present author also took part. Hence I would point out that the criticism of Prof. Van Baaren's views expressed here, should also be regarded as self-criticism; approbation of these views is of course to be taken as a mark of respect for the merits of Prof. Van Baaren's article.

REFERENCES

Argyle, Michael (1958), *Religious Behaviour*. London, Routledge & Kegan Paul.
Van Baal, J. (1971), *Symbols for Communication, an introduction to the anthropological study of religion*. Assen, Van Gorcum & Comp.
Van Baaren, Th. P. (1964), *Menschen wie wir, Religion und Kult der schriftlosen Völker*, Gütersloh: Gütersloher Verlagshaus Gerd Mohn.
— (1973), 'Science of Religion as a Systematic Discipline; Some Introductory Remarks,' in this volume, pp. 35 ff.
Brelich, A. (1970), 'Prolégomènes à une histoire des religions', in: H. C. Puech (ed.), *Histoire des Religions*, I. Paris, Editions Gallimard.
Douglas, Mary (1970), *Natural Symbols, Explorations in Cosmology*. London, Routledge & Kegan Paul.
Drijvers, H. J. W. (1973), 'Theory Formation in Science of Religion and the Study of the History of Religions,' Chap. 3, in this volume, pp. 57 ff.
Duncan, Hugh Dalziel (1969), *Symbols and Social Theory*. New York, Oxford University Press.
Elias, Norbert (1970), *Was ist Soziologie?* München, Juventa Verlag.
Geertz, Clifford (1958), 'Ethos, World-View and the Analysis of Sacred Symbols,' in *Antioch Review*, Winter 1957-1958.
— (1960), *The Religion of Java*. Glencoe, Ill., The Free Press.

— (1966), 'Religion as a Cultural System,' in Michael Banton (ed.), *Anthropological Appoaches to the Study of Religion*. London, Tavistock Publications.

Hempel, Carl G. (1965), *Aspects of Scientific Explanation and other Essays*. New York, Free Press.

Horton, Robin (1968), 'Neo–Tyloreanism: Sound sense or sinister prejudice,' pp. 625-634 in: *Man*, Vol. 3 no. 4 (Dec. 1968).

Jensen, Ad. E. (1951), *Mythos und Kult der Naturvölkern*. Wiesbaden, Franz Steiner Verlag.

Kluckhohn, Cl. (1954), 'Culture and Behavior,' in: C. Gardner Lindzey (ed.), *Handbook of Social Psychology*. Reading, Cambridge Mass., Addison Wesley.

Kroeber, A.L. and Kluckhohn, Cl. (1963), *Culture, A Critical Review of Concepts and Definitions*. New York, Vintage Books.

Leertouwer, L. (1967), 'Ritueel handelen,' in: *Vox Theologica* (Assen, Van Gorcum), 37 (Jan. 1967), pp. 12-27.

Van der Leeuw, G. (1956), *Phänomenologie der Religion*, 2. Aufl. Tübingen, Van den Hoeck & Ruprecht.

Lewin, Kurt (1951), *Field Theory in Social Science*. New York, Cartwright.

Mey, Harald (1972), *Field-theory: A study of its application on the social sciences*. London, Routledge & Kegan Paul.

Miller, Robert J. (1964), 'Cultures as Religious Structures,' pp. 91-101 in: June Helm (ed.), *Symposium on New Approaches to the Study of Religion*. Seattle, University of Washington.

Morgenstern, Christian (1952), *Alle Galgenlieder*, 3. Aufl. München, Insel Verlag.

Nadel, S. F. (1951), *The Foundations of Social Anthropology*. New York, Free Press.

Opp, K.D. (1970), *Methodologie der Sozialwissenschaften*. Hamburg, Rohwolt.

Radin, P. (1951), *Die Religiöse Erfahrung der Naturvölker*. Zürich-Stuttgart, Rhein Verlag.

Radin, P. (1957), *Primitive Religion, its Nature and Origin*. New York, Dover Publications.

Schneider, D.M. (1968), 'Some Muddles in the Models: or, How the System really Works,' in Michael Banton (ed.), *The Relevance of Models for Social Anthropology*. London, Tavistock Publications.

Spiro, Melford E. (1964), 'Religion and the Irrational,' in June Helm (ed.), *Symposium on New Approaches to the Study of Religion*. Seattle, University of Washington.

Spiro, Melford E. (1966), 'Religion: Problems of Definition and Explanation,' in Michael Banton (ed.), *Anthropological Approaches to the Study of Religion*. London, Tavistock Publications.

Teicher, Morton I. (1960), 'Windigo Psychosis, A Study of a Relationship between Belief and Behavior among the Indians of Northeastern Canada,' in V.F. Ray (ed.), *Proceedings of the 1960 Annual Spring Meeting of the American Ethnological Society*. Seattle, University of Washington.

Tennekes, J. (1971), *Anthropology, Relativism and Method*. Assen, Van Gorcum & Comp.

Turner, Victor (1967), *The Forest of Symbols, Aspects of Ndembu Ritual*. Ithaca-New York, Cornell University Press.

Wagenvoort, H. (1941), *Imperium. Studieën over het mana-begrip in zede en taal der Romeinen*. Amsterdam, H.J. Paris.

Widengren, Geo (1969), *Religionsphänomenologie*. Berlin, Walter de Gruyter & Co.

Worsley, P. (1957), *The Trumpet shall sound, a Study of Cargo Cults in Melanesia*. London, Macgibbon & Kee.

The Examination of Religious Concepts in Religious Anthropology

INTRODUCTION

Religious anthropology[1] has run into a blind alley. We see that the scientific treatment of the material of religious anthropology raises such problems that theory[2] formation can hardly make a proper start (cf. Geertz, 1965: 1-2). Religious anthropology does not dispose of a generally accepted terminological and conceptual apparatus. In what way material is gathered, interpreted, classified, etc. largely depends upon the particular school or trend to which one belongs. The differences between the many schools, trends, tendencies etc. of anthropology are often very fundamental. The structuralists attempt to find the 'organizing principles' of human thought and to represent these in formal models. The structural functionalists try to set up structural models of social institutions, and hope by this means to arrive at the formation of general rules for the functioning of these institutions. The 'social anthropologists' regard the individual as a negligible quantity in theory formation, while those who work with the 'cultural personality' take the individual as starting-point for theory formation. Mutual differences are often so great that a new name is desired for a particular scientific activity. Thus beside 'cultural anthropology' we find 'social anthropology', 'culturology', 'Kultur-anthropologie' and other terms.

1. By religious anthropology I understand that branch of cultural anthropology which is particularly concerned with religion.
2. In this paper I use 'theory' as: 'A system of logically connected, notably non-conflicting statements, views and concepts concerning some sphere of reality, which are formulated in such way that one can derive a hypothesis from them that can be tested.' (De Groot, 1970: 42)

These various schools and trends do indeed try to set up general theories, but the results are hardly overwhelming. Premature formalization often impairs the theories produced (cf. the culinary triangle of Lévi-Strauss). For the present it is best to look upon cultural anthropology as an attempt at science. We have to do with a field of research in which the development of science is being attempted by various means. One of the greatest problems here is to find concepts that can serve as basic elements for theory formation (cf. Schneider, 1965: 78).

Now the various schools of cultural anthropology are also concerned with religion. There is so little clarity, however, as to what religion really is, that frequently in describing the religion of a foreign culture its whole non-material aspect is, for safety's sake, included.

I shall therefore begin by considering the question: 'What is religion?' Obviously one's view of religion determines what can be regarded as religious concepts. Secondly, I shall treat the principal problem of this paper: 'How are religious concepts to be studied?' At the end of this paper I shall go into the problem of comparing religious concepts.

What is religion?

There are a good many religions, and the differences between them are often so great that we wonder whether it is right to call them all by the same generic name. Why do we give the name of religion to Buddhism and not to Marxism? Why do we call Christianity a religion and Roman Catholicism a church? How is the term of religion to be used? Is it possible to give a satisfactory definition of religion and if so, what are we going to do with such a definition? Now there are various kinds of definition, and it depends on the kind of research one is going to do which kind of definition one chooses. Very many definitions of religion have been given, but I shall confine myself here to a few of the most recent and the most important. These sufficiently illustrate how different approaches lead to totally different definitions.

Clifford Geertz defines religion as: 1) 'A system of symbols which acts to 2) establish powerful, pervasive and longlasting moods and motivations in men by 3) formulating conceptions of a general order of existence and 4) clothing these conceptions with such an aura of factuality that 5) the moods and motivations seem uniquely realistic.' (Geertz, 1965: 4). This rather formal definition is largely determined by Geertz's view of the task of the 'anthropological study of religion': 'The anthropological study of religion is therefore a two-stage operation: First an analysis of meanings embodied in the symbols which make up the religion proper (!) and second, the relating of these systems to social structural and psychological processes' (1965: 42). We see that for Geertz the system of symbols of a religion constitutes the starting-point of research.

Far otherwise Melford E. Spiro, who defines religion as: 'An institution of culturally patterned interaction with culturally postulated superhuman beings' (1965: 96). This definition thus turns upon the interaction of men and postulated superhuman beings.

Finally J. Milton Yinger defines religion as follows: 'Religion then can be defined as a system of beliefs and practices by means of which a group of people struggles with these ultimate problems of human life. It expresses their refusal to capitulate to death, to give up in the face of frustration, to allow hostility to tear apart their human associations' and he adds: 'The quality of being religious, seen from the individual point of view implies two things: first a belief that evil, pain, bewilderment and injustice are fundamental facts of existence; and second, a conviction that man can ultimately be saved from those facts' (1970: 7). This definition appears in the setting of a 'field theory of religion', developed by Milton Yinger in the same book (p. 82ff.). This field theory rests upon a functionalistic approach, in which religion is seen as a dynamic and open system in contrast with traditional functionalism which was usually based on static and closed systems. Also in the approach of Milton Yinger, however, the problem remains of defining basic elements from which the functional models are to be constructed.

We see how much these definitions differ. Geertz approaches religion rather formally as a cultural system, Spiro stresses interaction with superhuman beings, and Milton Yinger is concerned above all with the function of religion. These definitions all approach religion from different sides, so that they are not contradictory. It is the angle from which one views religion that determines what kind of definition one arrives at.

Every approach is based on a particular interpretation. Religion may be regarded as a system of classification, a system of signification, a pattern of interaction with superhuman beings etc. All these approaches result in different definitions and different methods of research. Looked at in this way the question 'What is religion really?' loses all meaning. Many approaches to religion are possible and there is no reason to elect one of them as the only correct approach. Yet we must not be too hasty with our conclusions. The various theoretical points of view aim at describing a particular sphere of reality in a particular manner. We are not engaged in a game of logic, but in trying to find a profitable and efficient way of examining a socio-cultural phenomenon, viz. religion. In how far the various theoretical points of departure, however, are to the purpose for the end in view is still, to put it mildly, a matter for discussion.

In the end, from these different theoretical standpoints, we yet again try to answer the question 'What is religion?' But now the question has lost its absolutistic character, and we take account of the fact that the answer depends to a very great extent on the manner in which religion is approached. It is the manner of approach which determines the object of examination and vice versa. Yet it is clear that one cannot call just anything religion. We go by the accepted meanings of the concept religion in this culture. More exact specification depends on the kind of research to be done.

Religious concepts are those concepts which play an important part in the conceptual framework of a particular religion. Whether one regards these concepts as religious again depends on the kind of research. In many cases conceptions of the soul can be regarded as religious, anthropological or psychological concepts as is most convenient. Here again the approach is decisive.

THE STUDY OF RELIGIOUS CONCEPTS

The religious concepts we examine always form part of a complex of religious conceptions and ideas. They may have an exactly defined place in a well thought-out theological system, or they may be extremely vague. In all cases, however, the problem of translation arises. How do we describe concepts of another culture in terms of our own culture? We do not do this through the medium of an objective terminological apparatus, but by the aid of concepts that play a great part in our own society: individual, community, etc.

P. Winch has already pointed out the great difficulties this involves. In examining foreign cultures we must realize that the socio-cultural sciences are to a great extent founded on a Western outlook on society and anthropology. In studying the anthropology of another culture, our possibilities are in fact determined by our own anthropology. This means that concepts such as 'individual' and 'community' may not be used in the description of foreign cultures without previous examination. The concept of 'individual' has had a long history with us, and is by no means so clearly defined as one might expect at first sight (cf. Elias, 1970). The fact that members of this culture are of opinion that they possess a conscious and a subconscious mind does not at all involve the utility of this distinction in describing Eskimo cultures.

All the same, the description of foreign cultures in terms of one's own culture is unavoidable. We must, then, consider the problem of translation when transferring concepts from one culture to another. How do we actually translate? In practice we do not work with definitions, as a simple example will show. To translate the French word *ciel*, the most important possiblities are 'sky' and 'heaven'. In translating one considers the context of the word, how 'sky' and 'heaven' are used in English etc. Finally one chooses the word that most fitly renders *ciel* in that particular context. More difficult is the word *esprit*. The words 'spirit', 'soul', 'mind', 'ghost' and so on differ entirely in value and meaning, and careful consideration is necessary.

Yet never does one first attempt to define the various terms. We find in practice that one can use words, develop a feeling for language, translate, etc. without being able to give definitions of the words one uses.

In religion we have a good deal to do with terms which are fairly generally agreed to be pretty vague: god, spirit, soul, etc. A French dictionary will offer us the following possible translations of *âme*: soul, mind, spirit, life, conscience, feeling; ghost; person; essence, etc., with additional special meanings such as bore (of a gun), sound-post (of a violin), core (of a bronze cast). These many meanings certainly do not make it clear what the place of the term *âme* has been in the Christian anthropology of Western culture. For that, extensive research would be required. Yet in practice a clear distinction is often felt in the use of such terms. One may speak of a village of a hundred souls, but not of a village of a hundred spirits. It would be an almost impossible task, however, to fix the limits between the words 'soul', 'spirit', 'conscience' and so on. The conception of the soul may play an important part in a man's personal religious life without his being able to give a clear conceptual definition of 'soul'.

We can see that the various meanings of *âme* given above are related, and that their mutual connexions can be described. The word *âme* obviously covers a fairly complex idea; 'soul' may be used with various meanings. In an expression such as 'poor soul' the shade of meaning is quite clear. It is only when one wishes to assign a well-defined meaning to the word 'soul' that one finds it troublesomely vague. The word simply has no unequivocal significance. In studying a concept of this kind, we must try to give an exact description of the use of the term. Such an analysis may then be summarized in a number of principal significations, giving structure to the understanding we have gained of the way the term is used. A short example may illustrate this.

The ideas about the soul are considerably more complicated with the Eskimo than with us. In their cultures we find different kinds of soul side by side. As we shall see, it is absolutely necessary to have some understanding of these conceptions if one would form a picture of these cultures, for they determine Eskimo anthropology and cosmology. As a rule we meet with a kind of soul that is the life force of a human being, often *inua* (lit.: 'his human person'), a soul that lives on after death. Often there is the *tarnik* (derived from a root tar-, lit.: dark) and the *ateq* ('name').

The principal meanings of the word *inua* are: owner, human soul, manifestation as a human being or in human form, spirit, mask. Most spirits can be called *Inua*. The animals also have an inua. The various meanings are interlinked in a number of ways. The masks in Alaska are often called *inuat* because they represent spirits or animals with their human soul. The three most important spirits (of the sea, the air and the moon) were originally human and are called *inuat*. Stones, rivers, and other inanimate objects also often have an *inua*.

While inanimate objects mostly have an *inua*, only living beings have a *tarnik*. As a rule the *tarnik* is a miniature edition of a animal or a human being, and is situated in an internal organ (kidney, liver, groin and so on). This *tarnik* is the seat of health. Its loss usually results in illness and ultimately in death. This soul functions in the shamanistic seance, for it is the soul which leaves the *shaman* when he is in trance. It is also the soul which is usually the target of sorcery.

The name links its bearer with all those who share it, and particularly with the namesake from whom he received the name. The dead support their living namesakes, so that it is important to be well provided with names. It may happen that a man antagonizes the souls of his dead namesakes. In that case he had best provide himself with another name. The ideas about life after death are on the whole fairly vague. Often contradictory views exist side by side. The dead always live on, however, and the living must reckon with the fact, especially during the first days after death has taken place, while the dead person's soul is still close to the corpse. A slight transgression of the rules and prohibitions to be observed may be enough to change the dead person into a malevolent spirit seeking to avenge itself upon the transgressors, and sometimes even upon the whole community.

It is clear that these conceptions of the soul, only roughly sketched here, result in a totally different anthropology from our Western one. Like men, the animals have a human soul (*inua*). Often they live in villages somewhere in human shape, just like people. In a sense animals do not rank lower than men. They must be treated with respect. Otherwise their souls will turn against us.

The *tarnik*, then, is the seat of health. Illness and misfortune are usually ascribed to a spiritual cause. A man's well-being is intimately linked with his relation to the spirits and souls that inhabit his world. A poor catch, bad weather, etc. are not blamed upon climatological factors, but upon transgression of a complex of prescripts and prohibitions that rules these cultures.

The name *binds* its bearer so closely to his namesakes that one cannot speak of a 'self' in the sense of our culture. The name permeates a person's whole being, giving him specific qualities and defects.

We have to do here with an outlook upon the world and an anthropology in which the fundamental concepts are very different from those in our own culture. Most Eskimo, however, are no more able to give a clear description of their 'souls' than we are of our own. When they do proffer such a description, it is usually an explanation ad hoc, which must be weighed with a critical judgement.

To study these ideas, we must begin with our own general ideas (soul, spirit, religion, etc.). We can make an overall analysis of their content, as the Groninger Working-Group has done for religion. This gives us a rational starting-point for research. Naturally such a religious anthropological study will as a rule have to be preceded by serious study of the culture as a whole. The various ways the term in question is used must then be examined, and the variations in that use (often factors such as place, time, social group or stratum, situation and so on will greatly influence such variations).

Research of this kind will usually result in a fairly extensive description of the variations in the use and the function of the term in its own culture. In the translation the manner in which the concept is handled in the foreign culture must be carefully compared with the way one's own concept is treated in one's own culture. Thus we not only gain a delicate insight in the meaning and function of the foreign concept, but our own concepts also deepen their content and shades of meaning through constant comparison. We come to a better understanding of the way we ourselves use these concepts and the way our own world is determined by them.

THE COMPARISON OF RELIGIOUS CONCEPTS

We have seen from the above that we study different cultures with the same concepts (spirit, god, etc.). This also offers the possibility of comparing concepts with each other. In this great care must be exercised, for it is in the comparing of concepts that matters often go awry.

First of all it should be stated in what point it is proposed to compare the concepts. Secondly, it must be clear from what theoretical viewpoint this is done. Every distinction, every classification presupposes a more or less detailed theoretical point of view. In religious anthropology we use a great many distinctions. We distinguish between spirits and gods, between believers and unbelievers, between shamans and priests, etc. The theoretical view-points on which these distinction are based, however, are mostly somewhat nebulous.

It is indeed extremely difficult to work out these theoretical points of view. Theory formation is not something that can take place in a vacuum. It must be guided by a question concerning a definite subject. We shall have to ask ourselves why, i.e. with what purpose, we are really studying religion. The structure of religious anthropological research depends upon how this question is answered.

Of course no unequivocal answer is to be expected. Yet the distinctions we make indicate that we already have certain theoretical points of view that we wish to work out further. Whether these will constitute a basis for theory formation, however, is an open question. In the physical sciences the value of a theory usually rests upon its practical utility and not upon the truth it is supposed to contain. The theories developed so far in religious anthropology rarely have a practical application, and are moreover difficult to test. Thus their value is still at best uncertain.

Now one cannot force theory formation. There must be an equilibrium between theory formation on one side and empirical research on the other. If we neglect theory, the research loses its scientific character, but if we proceed to premature formalization, we end up with pseudo-science and lose contact with the social reality we are studying. The formation of theory and empirical research are therefore indissolubly linked. Theory formation must be based on an careful study of the concepts with the aid of which we describe foreign cultures. Only with the utmost precaution may these concepts be detached from their cultural context and compared with one another. In any case we must pay great attention to the way we use our own concepts. Any attempt at theory formation that disregards this problem is doomed to failure.

REFERENCES

Elias, Norbert (1970), *Was ist Soziologie?* München, Juventa Verlag.
Geertz, Clifford (1965), 'Religion as a Cultural System,' pp. 1-46 in Michael Banton (ed.), *Anthropological Approaches to the Study of Religion*. London, Tavistock Publications.

De Groot, A.D. (1970⁵), *Methodologie. Grondslagen van onderzoek en denken in de gedragswetenschappen*. Den Haag, Mouton. English transl.: *Methodology. Foundations of Inference and Research in the Behavioral Sciences*. The Hague, Mouton (1969).

Schneider, D.M. (1965), 'Some Muddles in Models,' pp. 25-85 in Michael Banton (ed.), *The Relevance of Models for Social Anthropology*. London, Tavistock Publications.

Spiro, Melford E. (1965), 'Religion: Problems of Definition and Explanation,' pp. 85-126 in Michael Banton (ed.), *Anthropological Approaches to the Study of Religion*. London, Tavistock Publications.

Yinger, J. Milton (1970), *The Scientific Study of Religion*. London, The Macmillan Comp.

Research on Meaning in Religion

In the course of his work the historian of religions professionally en-
counters the singular problem of 'meaning'. Especially if he works on
one of the living world religions, he is compelled to admit that a religious
faith comprises a view on life and reality either as something meaningful
or as referring to something meaningful. The question, then, is legitimate
how a student of religion should proceed in order to grasp such a view
intellectually and so to arrive at an insight into the way in which his
fellow-man looks at life and reality, and what kinds of meaning he thereby perceives. Now for any research on what things mean to someone or
to a community, it is important to know both whether the people
concerned have a religion and what this religion as such possibly means
to them. For the meaning of a particular religious datum for someone is
immediately connected with the overall meaning of the corresponding
religion — or with its possible meaninglessness — to that person. And
what is said here of an individual person holds equally true for a concrete
community, culture or civilisation. As soon as the question is raised what
it holds to be meaningful, an enquiry should be made whether there is a
religion and if so, what religion and what kinds of meaning this religion
may confer on life and reality for this community, culture or civilisation.
So any cultural research will encounter the phenomenon of religion
and, more concretely, the problem what a particular religion means to a
particular culture. The present paper intends to discuss one aspect of this
general problem.

Although the problem itself is not new, present-day scholarship seems
to allow a new way of treating it. In many respects the present time
appears to be more favourable to an impartial study of religion in
general, and its meaning in particular, than former periods could allow.
Negatively, religions are much less studied according to the received

ideas of Western society, since very little here is any longer held to be self-evident. Positively, many questions with regard to religion, which formerly had been solved in advance or which simply were not put, purposely or by implication, can at present be formulated, since very little now is held to be beyond interrogation and questioning. It is in this spirit that we want to discuss some aspects of a primary datum of the history of religions: that within a given culture certain things have a meaning for certain people, and that within a given context such a meaning may have a religious quality for a particular group or person. The question then is legitimate, whether and how such meanings, and especially the religious ones, should be studied by the scholar who has chosen this as his field of investigation.

Meaning. The problem of the meaning of religious data is specified here as that of the meaning of these data for the people concerned. It is realised that the objective classification, study and interpretation of given facts necessarily leads to the problem of their meaning, in the sense indicated. This problem is evident in the renewed interest in hermeneutical questioning, and one finds it also expressed in booktitles like *The Meaning of Religion*, by W. Brede Kristensen (1960), and *The Meaning and End of Religion*, by W. Cantwell Smith (1963). It is especially in the latter study that the question of the meaning of religious data, here specifically those contained in a given religious tradition, for those who are concerned with them or committed to them — that is to say their 'subjective' meaning or significance — receives much attention. This was less the case in what we would like to call the 'classical' type of phenomenology of religion, where research on meaning in religion to a large extent coincided with the search for objective patterns, coming down to basic mental or philosophical structures in the world of religious phenomena.

The question which we put here is of a slightly different nature, namely to what extent we can grasp 'subjective' meanings, that is to say the significance of certain concrete religious data to certain people. In thus asking what someone else 'means with' what he expresses, or what something 'means for' someone other than ourselves, we understand the concept of 'meaning' in a specific sense. And so in what follows we shall use the word 'meaning' in this restricted sense of the contents of 'subjective meaning' as 'meaning contents' for someone. The word 'significance' refers thereby to its objective side, its source, and the word 'signification' indicates a specific reference which a significance or a meaning makes with regard to a signified reality as a *tertium datum* in the signifying process. If we say, for instance: 'nature means happiness to Peter', the *meaning* which imparts itself to Peter is that of 'happiness', while it is 'nature' that, to Peter, has the *significance* of happiness. And if we say: 'nature means the happiness of paradise to Peter', 'nature' has the *signification* of 'happiness of paradise' by referring specifically to a paradisal reality. Much confusion can be avoided if we separate, moreover, methodically and rigorously all research on 'subjective meanings', with which we are concerned here, from that on meanings as they may exist in themselves, metaphysically, or meanings as they may exist for the scholar either personally or as categories of his scholarly interpretation.

In our interpretations we always attribute meanings to facts; consequently, there are no 'pure' but only interpreted facts. Yet we must methodically distinguish our interpretations, as meanings, from the facts themselves. On the assumption that man is a kind of being that attributes and receives meaning, our contention is that, when meaning and fact are to be distinguished analytically, within human culture things always have both a factual aspect and a meaning aspect. It is, by the way, only in a civilisation like the modern Western one, impregnated by science and its objectifications, that not only in thought but also in experience a separation between both aspects could be made, a consequence of which was the development of scholarly research and of technology.

This very distinction between fact and meaning poses the question of meaning in a new way. Indeed, the actuality of meaning research has to do, on one hand, with the immensely increased factual knowledge which we command at present and, on the other hand, with a certain crisis in Western civilisation where older accepted meaning giving patterns and systems apparently are in process of dissolving themselves, whatever be the reason of it. And the present interest in research on meanings for *others* than ourselves has to do, as we will show, not only with natural curiosities, but also with the gradual emergence of the category of 'the other'. This is an important factor in any interest in knowing the culture, religion, and 'life world' of other people.

Meaning research. Our concern is the meaning, religious and otherwise, which particular phenomena turn out to have had or to have under certain conditions for certain people, religious expression being a particular case. Our contention is that, among the various disciplines dealing with hermeneutical or semiological problems and which have to work together here, a contribution can be made by a 'new style'phenomenological research in so far as this views human expressions, including the religious ones, with reference to human intentions. The old adagio of phenomenology, *back to the facts*, is to be reformulated here as: *back to the basic intentions.*

Like other disciplines, phenomenology of religion has had its history including the phases of birth, childhood and ripening. If some scholars tend to reject this approach altogether, we for our part rather prefer to accompany its further growth, to put limits to an excessive subjectivism and then to enjoy its potential contribution to scholarship. For our purpose this contribution would lie in the fact that it deals with spheres of human reality which we would like to call its areas of significance: integral parts of man's life and creativity, but at first sight impressively irrational. Subjects like intersubjectivity and imagination, religion and art, are, as far as their significance is concerned, beyond pure facticity and we are here put explicitly before the problem of that significance. This realm with its expressions has a direct relevance for the question of meaning and can be made subject to phenomenological analysis. For such meaning research, however, classical phenomenology of religion will have to restyle itself to become a tool of research on actual human reality. In the first place the meaning of given data for given people should be the focus of interest. A phenomenologist thereby tries to analyse intentionality structures in a way which is parallel to that of a röntgenologist X-raying the human body to its bones, a psychoanalyst laying bare the emotions of the unconscious, or a structural anthropologist analysing social reality to find its structures. In the second place the search should be for a coherent hypothesis or a theory in order to solve a problem connected with a set of data; such a hypothesis or theory has then to be verified in subsequent empirical research. To study 'religion' in this phenomenological perspective would be to reconstruct religious meanings on the basis of the available documentary materials, with particular attention paid to the intentionalities contained in them. As we will show later, to ask what they mean or meant then mainly comes down to the question: what was or is intended?

The fundamental datum under consideration here is that different things can have a similar meaning to different peoples and cultures, and that different peoples and cultures can attribute to the same thing very different meanings, with often complicated interconnections and justifications. Especially when these meanings acquire a religious quality or connotation, and certainly if they are seen in what is commonly called a 'religious light', the factual aspects of things are overshadowed by their significance aspects. As we will see later, on closer analysis many of such meanings appear to be immediately related with basic problems with which human existence, collectively or individually, is confronted, be it as such or be it in particular conditions.

Within any given society there are a number of data which have, beyond their implicit 'everyday life' meaning and beyond their functional — technical, economic, social, and so on — meaning, some kind of 'surplus value' which strikes the outsider through its gratuitousness if not apparent uselessness, and which distinguishes itself thereby from utility and everyday life meanings. Part of such data are, in terms of the culture concerned, called 'religious'; they generally contain significations relating to realities different from the verifiable one. Others refer to what we are used to call art, play, morality, intersubjectivity or just free imagination, whereby not only the meaning aspect predominates over the factual aspect, but whereby also the surplus meaning, at least on certain occasions, predominates over the other meaning patterns of that particular action or behavior, so that they may appear as being 'meaningless' in terms of utility and 'everyday life'. Such surplus values are often accompanied by strong emotional and physical involvements, be it as tension or be it as relaxation.

A methodological problem here is evident. If the nature and conditions of such behavior, and of other expressions of this kind, can be studied as facts, and if that already may often not be easy, it is still much more difficult to grasp what, in such expressions, people are looking for, or from what they are trying to free themselves: and to grasp this both in terms of what it means to them and so that the interpreter himself can understand it. Indeed, very often the real meanings appear not to be conscious as 'meanings', but rather to be lived as self-evident, unquestioned truths. Speaking metaphorically, it appears that, in the case of such expressions, something like a channel is opened up, through which some kind of special significance is transmitted and can be received, and which causes the significance that these expressions have for those concerned. In more philosophical language one may say that certain words, actions or data become phenomena signifying 'transcendence' on certain occasions for certain people. It would be through this serious or casual reference to transcendence, to 'something different', that people are lifted beyond their daily life world with its common sense, norms, utilities and boundaries. By signifying another reality, religion in particular provides a 'double bottom' to human life as it is lived.

In this dialectic of every-day and other meaning, the religious meanings, as far as they are expressed, often cannot but be 'meaningless' or sheer 'nonsense' in terms of the common-sense world of meaning. On the level of experience, one observes involvements of particular significance, which lift people above the level of common-sense experience. On the level of expression, one observes certain particularly strong meaning expressions, whereby something which may be ordinary for others, has an extra-ordinary, e.g. revelatory, significance for those involved. We think, for instance, of 'mystical' experiences of revelation and ecstasy, or of the 'normal' experience of religious conscience.

Speaking descriptively, a religious meaning appears to be of an existential nature, i.e. it applies to man's individual or communal existence; because of this existential nature, it only exceptionally can be found through direct question and answer. The fact that religious expressions occur in certain situations, and that they make explicit only a part of their ideational contents while the greater part remains implicit, makes for the rule that the greater part of them must be interpreted by inference and by intentional analysis.

It is worthwhile to pay attention to some conditions under which this meaning research has been carried out, for instance, in the first half of this century, as far as the basic assumptions are concerned. One specific theological orientation and one specific way of theological thinking could not but have its consequences for this sort of descriptive work.

As soon as, theologically or otherwise, one sort of direct access to the absolute is postulated, this has not only consequences for the student's outlook and vision on religion as a whole, for instance as a phenomenon in itself with its own particular constitutive elements and as a value category in itself. Such a view will also imply an interest in particular sets of religious phenomena which are studied in isolation, to the neglect of other phenomena or of their interconnections. It may also hamper progressive questioning on the basis of human reason alone, and thwart genuine philosophical reflection in favour of revelation for its own sake with a bracketing of critical reason as last criterion of judgment. Among theologians, phenomenology of religion, unfortunately, appears to have functioned less to promote authentic philosophical or theological investigations than to lead, too often, to making certain theological or philosophical pronouncements on the level of conviction rather than that of enquiry and reflection. In the humanities, on the other hand, the phenomenological suspense of judgement was applied too often in such a way that religious phenomena became in practice objects of literary and historical research without too much attention being paid to their significance for the people who lived with them, or to the evident claims with regard to truth and reality as they are contained in material varying from myths to sacred scriptures. Such a neglect of the appeal contained in religious phenomena regarding life as experienced in different cultures and societies may have profound theological reasons: if only theological truth is on the market, the authentic quest for truth as held by others becomes easily frustrated. And if one thinks of the work of a scholar like Gerardus van der Leeuw, admirable as it may be, one has to avow that a phenomenology of religion, if put under a specific theological protection or guardianship, cannot but find itself unable to gain access to problems which are beyond the magic circle of its protector: as every student of magic and religion should theoretically also know!

Among students of religion, philosophy has been identified for a long time with Kantian and Hegelian thought. One of the consequences of this particular kind of philosophy of religion has been, apart from its implied specific critique of knowledge, an idealistic trend throughout the study of religion. There easily arose a conceptual ideation of reality rather than an investigation of reality in terms of rational hypotheses

and theories based on empirical data. The study of religion thus threatened
to be reduced to the study of either a pure idea or a pure experience,
whereby the term 'phenomenology of religion' could readily be used
for such an enterprise. The unfortunate consequence was, that in what
we call classical phenomenology of religion religious facts and phenomena
became isolated from other facts and phenomena, and that, both in
research and teaching, students of religion tended to isolate themselves
from those of their colleagues whose task it is to study other aspects of
human reality. This may account for the very restricted interaction
which there has been between classical phenomenology of religion and
the empirical disciplines, for instance of the social sciences, and also for
the relatively little assistance that the phenomenological syntheses could
give to those who had to deal with religion as an empirical reality.
This situation influenced negatively, for instance, the study of Islam,
where a neat separation between 'religious' and 'non-religious' facts
cannot be made. It also had consequences for the study of Eastern religions, the 'spirituality' of which was often esteemed to be greater than
that of Western religion, through an idealization which to a great
extent arose from an internal criticism of the empirical reality of one's
own self and society. Such deformations may belong to the past now. In
the present situation, both in religious and non-religious quarters, there
appears to be less difficulty in appreciating religion, be it one's own or an
alien one, simply as a human phenomenon.

Classical phenomenology of religion, as represented in past genera-
tions in the Netherlands by scholars like P.D. Chantepie de la Saussaye,
W. Brede Kristensen and G. van der Leeuw, had some other weaknesses
which played a role in its meaning research. Basically it was looking for
objective structures in the realm of religious phenomena and worked
much more at designing syntheses than at doing analytical research.
Methodologically, unfortunately, there was too little search for the
criteria under which an intuitioned 'evidence', had to fall to be counted
as valid. The result has been a relatively weak selfcriticism within the
discipline where the norms were not clear enough, and this indeed was
conducive to appealing to the 'irrational' side of religion. The consequence has been that certain personal convictions could be launched
and that certain value statements could be asserted without justification,

or just be implied. So, in this field in particular, much work that was done 'above the ground' with regard to religion was fed by thoughts on the subject which existed 'underground'. Instead of claiming to know what religion essentially is, of all investigators the student of religion should rather admit that he, precisely, does not know what religion is. And if he pretends to know it, his phenomenology of religion easily becomes a schematization of religious phenomena.

There are, of course, a number of very real practical limitations to *any* phenomenological work in the field of religion, which have their repercusions in meaning research. We mention here only three of them. First, we have to do with concrete data, and specifically with data which are religiously qualified; consequently, 'religion' as such, not as a working definition but as a reality, is an extrapolation from the phenomena. Second, since we have to do with phenomena that have some absolute connotations for the people concerned, there is the ever present risk that the discipline itself or one of its students comes within the grasp of such an absolute, often by sheer fascination. The result may be an absolutized idea on the part of the scholar, which leads to a misrepresentation of reality; or even the discipline itself might tend to absolutize itself, to become a sort of new religious ideology. And third, no intelligent student of religion can be unaware of the ambiguous role of any religion in man's grasping truth or illusion, becoming alienated or rooted, in man's quest or escape, in his fulfilling or forsaking life. To what extent such problems too may become subject of phenomenological enquiry must remain undiscussed here. And there are many more limitations to phenomenological research on religion.

On the whole, what we call 'classical' phenomenology of religion has interpreted 'meaning' in terms of connections or structures between religious phenomena or, exceptionally, between religious and non-religious phenomena. The search was for deeper connections described as patterns, types, ideal types, and so on. The 'new style' phenomenological research in religion interprets 'meaning' rather in terms of connections existing between concrete people and those data which have a religious significance for them. The phenomenologist is concerned with ways in which man experiences reality, religiously or not, and how he gives expression to this experience in word and action; he asks what significances play a role for man and under what circumstances. Basically, he will interrogate his material in the light of questions like these; when he studies religion as a human expression, his quest is for what has been expressed. And this is a problem of 'meaning', specifically 'religious meaning'.

Subjective meaning. The problem of meaning in cultures which are larger than tribal cultures, and in religions which stretch over various cultures like the present-day world religions, presents a special case. For these religions explicitly want to guide people who are living in completely different circumstances, and with totally different individual and communal life patterns, precisely in terms of meaning. They intend to be instrumental in giving transcendent references, if not salvation, in view of man's going from the meaningless to the meaningful. Their claim is that they have universal validity; they are units of meaning or systems of signification which embrace different times and places in a particular way. Now the local conditions of different communities which belong to such a universal religion can be studied. But it is quite difficult to grasp then what these different people really have in common or in what way there is a real experience among them of belonging to one great overall-community.

The structure of a tribal religion can be studied within the context of the social life of the tribe in question. But the way in which the structure of world religions like Islam or Christianity is to be studied has to be different. Assuming that such large religious systems engrave themselves to a smaller or larger extent upon the different cultural settings where they are acknowledged, our task is to try to analyse the fundamental orientations and religious views which they provide to people. As belief, value and action systems which function in different local cultures, they must be supposed to offer interpretations of the meaning of life and reality, which are beyond the context of a particular culture. The same holds true for the basic choices or options which they provide to man for the better solution of certain life problems. So it is necessary to study not only the religious systems in themselves, but also the meaning they have to particular people in particular circumstances. This 'subjective meaning' has to do with an *appeal* which is contained in such systems.

As a consequence, especially in the world religions, which have also been articulated in abstract thought, the question of 'subjective meaning' imposes itself insidiously on the student as a problem of meaning research.

The significance of facts like rituals, myths and doctrines for those who are involved in them, is not a 'fact' in the same sense as those mentioned: it is a datum contained in facts, but itself of a non-factual character. So the investigation of this significance or subjective meaning has often been eliminated from scholarly research, in so far as this restricted itself to the investigation of facts in the strict sense of the word and to establishing causal relations between them. However, research on meaning became a problem when further investigations showed functional and finalistic relations existing between given facts. It was evident thereby that the study of the meaning which something has to someone cannot be separated from a study of the concrete situation and of the general context in which such a person or group perceives such a meaning. What we want to do in the phenomenological study of subjective meaning is to pursue this line of investigation.

Fruitful research on subjective meanings, indeed, can only be carried out in a restricted number of specific favourable cases. We just mention three of the numerous conditions which must be satisfied in order that such a research on subjective meaning can take place. First, there should be sufficient materials available; not only those containing the direct or indirect expressions of such a meaning, but also others pertaining to the material and ideological background and the context of these expressions. Second, the expressions should be such that they can be interpreted as a human self-understanding or a human testimony. In other words, the materials should not be too dispersed to show certain structures and certain intentions, with regard to which the details become intelligible. Third, there should be available other data allowing (re)construction of the overall idea-system within which such expressions have their place and to which their 'meaning' is related. Conditions like these are perhaps best satisfied in the study of present-day living religion.

Under such conditions the research done on ideologies, on belief, value and action systems, both on a theoretical level and in the analysis of concrete societies and their religions, can be continued in the direction of research on 'subjective meaning'. Important thereby is the fact of the self-evident validity of such ideologies, or at least of great parts of them, for the people concerned: they are simply not put into question in a fundamentally critical way, and their meaning is simply available to the adherents who may 'receive' it. This fact of self-evident validity may be explained by the presence of some justification of the system on the basis of something held to be absolute; any negation of such an 'absolute' would take place only with difficulty and would logically imply a 'change of religion'. Apart from the history and the structure of the ideology itself, the question is open to investigation why at certain places and times certain parts of the ideology had or have significance for certain people, and why at other places and times specific other parts are felt to be significant. We must assume that there is an appeal coming from the system, an appeal which may lead to openness and acceptance on the part of the adherents; this openness may lead to a subjective reflection and 'meaning' and may result in a new way of man's understanding himself. The reception of this meaning by some and not by other people, the difference of significance of the same item to different people, and the different responses to this significance at different times and places while it is yet fully acknowledged, are important problems both for concrete research and for general theory formation. The basic methodological question here is how we can analyse the ideational contents of a given religious expression or phenomenon in such a way that the meaning which it has for the people concerned as well as the appeal which is behind it, can be ascertained. We come here to the problem of understanding.

Understanding. The problem of 'understanding' has been and is a central issue in the study of religion, and certainly in phenomenology of religion. We cannot deal here with the many ways in which this problem has been tackled from different sides. It is here approached from the actual situation of the student whose task it is to search for the meaning of human religious expressions. This situation can be defined as being that of a researcher A, who is confronted:

– either with certain facts p, q, r etc., which are direct or indirect expressions of an unknown person X, or of an unknown group of people X, Y, Z etc.,

– or with a certain person B, or a certain group of people B, C, D etc.,
who produced the known facts a, b, c etc., and who may express
themselves in the future by the facts x, y, z etc.

In our research we have then to conclude:

– in the first case from the facts p, q, r to the unknown person X or the
unknown group X, Y, Z etc.,
– in the second case from the facts a, b, c etc. to the person(s) B (C, D
etc.) vice versa; as well as from both the facts a, b, c etc. and the person(s)
B (C, D etc.) to the possible future facts x, y, z etc., which may, by the
way, very well be expressed by B (C, D etc.) under our own direct or
indirect influence.

Although in both cases we seek the meaning of facts, it goes without
saying that our procedure and our possible results will be completely
different in the two cases. The research of religious meanings in past
religion is fundamentally different from such research in present-day
religion. We say that this is the difference between historical research (in
our case using mainly texts as evidence) and anthropological or sociological
research (using mainly direct observation and interrogation). But we can
also learn from this difference about the ways in which meaning is expressed, and the ways in which meanings can be understood. Let us
analyse the situation a bit further and thereby show the task of the
scholar.

In both cases we are dealing with religious expressions, or religious
phenomena which were or are meaningful to one person or to a group;
this implies a direct relationship between that person or group and his
or its religious expression, or with regard to a given religious phenomenon.

Now at this point there is a riddle: is there something beyond the
man and his religious expression, say his prayer, or beyond the religious
phenomenon, say the statue, and the man before it? Of course this question remains a riddle; it may even be a riddle to the man himself. Yet,
from a phenomenological point of view something can be said, and we
have here an example of the usefulness of phenomenology. If we study
religion as a human reality, we can state that a prayer has a meaning and
that kneeling before a statue has a meaning. We may even state that we
have access, be it partial, to this meaning, through the words contained in
the prayer or through the behavior before the statue. And on any further

analysis it becomes evident that there is an intention, or more than one intention, contained in this meaning: the intention of the man who prays in this particular way, or who adores in this particular way. What the phenomenological researcher is after, is to uncover, within the meaning of the prayer, the intention(s) which made this man pray, and which took shape in the manner in which he prayed. A phenomenological analysis of such a prayer, or of a set of prayers by the same person, can, on the condition that there is enough material, make us guess to a satisfactory degree, behind the meaning of the words, the intention(s) of the man. The same holds true for the adoration of the statue: in both cases an analysis in depth should be able to bring to light a whole religious universe, and it may even give a glimpse of the 'intended object' of the man, that is to say that sort of reality to which the man addressed himself.

Perhaps we can summarize the above, which is enough to clarify what we mean by saying that the phenomenologist tries 'to understand religious meaning'. Any religious expression or any behavior with regard to a religious phenomenon can be read not only in terms of its literal meaning or its factual behavior, but also in terms of one or more human intentions which produced the expression or the behavior as such, and which then took its actual shape in the words or the elements of this specific expression and behaviour. It is assumed that, in addition to their direct meaning, these words and elements 'refer' to a directed intention. The actual job of phenomenological understanding is to guess such intentions. Theoretically we must assume that beyond the immediate relationship between the man and his expression there is a still more direct relationship between the man and his intention: that the expression is meaningful because of what the man wanted to express, or what he had in view when expressing himself. Also, that the intention — and certainly the 'intended object' — is not immediately given to the researcher, but 'hinted at' or 'designated' by the facts to which he has immediate access. And, finally, that it is the trans-empirical, 'transcendent' reference of such facts which makes them what we would call, at least from a phenomenological point of view, 'religious'. That the grasping of the intention and of the intentional object is and remains 'scholarly guesswork' is clear.

Let us come back now to the situation of the student. If he has to deal, as in the first case mentioned above, with certain facts of unknown persons, he has only a limited number of checks on any hypothesis on his part, and these checks are all indirect. The unknown persons cannot be interrogated, and any extension or correction of given interpretations is dependent upon new facts which one may chance to find and use, and which may or may not have a connection with the already given facts. The absence of persons implies that no new facts — expressions — can be produced, and that the interpretation of the existing facts depends to a great extent on the questions which the researcher wants to resolve with the help of these facts. Yet under certain favorable circumstances he will be able to detect 'intentions' by recognizing the 'reference' character of his facts, should he want to 'read' at that level.

But there is another feature of the situation of the scholar in the first given case, that of given facts of unknown persons. The facts which are at his disposal, are rarely direct religious expressions of individuals or groups who made them themselves. In by far the most cases he is dealing with phenomena, like statues, liturgies, myths and rituals, with which such individuals and groups found themselves confronted, but which were made by others. And it is therefore much more difficult, because of their 'objective' character, to guess the intentions both of those who made them and certainly of those who were confronted with them. So much work on religious phenomena is done in order to know the 'externals', and in the few cases that some sort of search for intentions has been carried out there often was the pitfall of finding 'hidden wisdom and secrets' which the researcher himself had presumed he would find. Yet a phenomenological analysis of the still available texts, monuments, works of art, and so on, with their context and background, may be able to discover intentions behind the given phenomenon. Our main argument for the existence of such intentions would be, first that such phenomena were made at all, and second that all of them have something to do with powers, spirits, gods and goddesses, that is to say intended objects 'par excellence'. Furthermore, that it is through the intentions that one discovers a basic religious structure.

We come now to the situation of the student in the second case. Because of the presence of both facts and persons he has here a most valuable check at his disposal. Even in his absence new expressions will continue to take place and new facts will be produced, which he will be able to use. And in the presence of such persons, he can maintain conversations, put questions like 'what do you mean?', or just live with the people in question and be attentive. He can hardly ignore the human reference of the material he studies. But what, in our sense, is most important, is that in the case of living religions the student deals with people expressing themselves, in some way. And so he can see the other side of religion, which necessarily remains a closed book to the historian: the immediate reactions of living people to religious phenomena, and the occurrence of religious expressions which are not necessarily put into literature. But for all this, the task of guessing what it all means to the people concerned is none the easier. Those involved do not see themselves, their expressions, nor their life stations as facts in the way the researcher sees them. Asked about their meaning, they may be too surprised at the question itself to be able to answer, or they will give stereotyped, traditional answers. Most probably, however, hardly anyone asked will answer that something might be meaningless: even if he were embarrassed at being unable to explain the implicit meaning.

There is, however, another factor which complicates this research. The task being to investigate the meaning and to uncover the intentions of religious expressions and of phenomena which are religious to a people living with them, the student becomes more or less involved in that a number of things in the community become meaningful to him. In history this may happen in the study, in the social sciences this can and probably will happen in reality. We have to stop here without going on to develop a theory on different sorts and kinds of involvements and possible commitments, of which some may be positive depending on the results obtained.

We have said before, that understanding the meaning of a direct religious expression implies an understanding of what this expression meant to the person concerned, and that the core of the meaning, phenomenologically speaking, is the intention which brought about the expression. We have also said that this intention cannot be grasped immediately, but only indirectly, by using elements of the expression as 'references' or 'hints'. Now in our opinion the whole interpretative effort on the part of the scholar, looking for what we called the religious meaning, the intention and the intended object of the religious expression, implies the constitution of a mental universe on his side: a universe which is aligned upon what appears to be the basic problems of the culture or the person studied, and which also shows the direction in which an over-coming of these problems is looked for. So the scholar attempts to reconstitute the existential problems and the transcendent references or openings which lay behind the specific expression he is investigating. The success of the effort to understand thereby largely depends on his ability to constitute, at least for a moment, the religious universe to which the expression testifies, and to interpret this expression in view of what is 'transcendent' in that universe, or what we may call the 'religious back-ground' of that universe. We would hope that this hypothesis may be worthwhile enough to be considered. Several times the attempt has been made to state what the understanding of a religious expression actually is. Our way has been to offer here a phenomenological analysis of such understanding, and this method appears to be the more adequate since the heart and core of any phenomenology is the understanding of mean-ing. A discussion along phenomenological lines will be helpful to elucidate the problem of how we can understand religion at all, and how we should proceed in practice.

Phenomena. We would like to extend now what we said about the under-standing of direct religious expressions to those religious phenomena of a so-called 'objective' nature, such as rituals, symbols, liturgies, statues, with which individuals and groups are confronted. First we must find out, what religious phenomena existed in a given society at a given time. It is then our task to investigate the meaning which these phe-nomena had in a given society, or at least for certain groups or even individuals in that society. Again, it is an investigation of meaning, but in this case not of direct expressions, but of given religious facts with which people were or are in relationship. This is a more complicated problem, because many of these religious facts continued to exist in successive cultural periods, in which their meanings changed: until they were abolished at a moment when they were considered to be meaningless or just 'wrong', 'false'. Here again there are sharp differences between the treatment of past and of living religion. In the first case, the people to whom these phenomena meant something are absent and only rarely do we have testimonies about that meaning they experienced. Our understanding starts here with what the data about these phenomena convey to us with regard to their meaning. However, under favorable circumstances, that is to say when a relatively great number of such data is available, and especially if we have texts at our disposal, we may be able to reconstruct or 'constitute' the corresponding religious universe and get an idea of certain religious meanings and intentions connected with these data: even though direct religious expressions are absent. Etymological, semantic, and historical research has indeed given positive results in this direction, sometimes supplemented with the help of comparative research, and with present-day findings of sociology and anthropology.

But it will be clear that the study of living religion will prove to be particularly fruitful for such meaning research, because of the presence of:

a) The self-expressions which we discussed before;
b) The religious phenomena which can be studied as they developed historically with changing meanings, as just mentioned;
c) The people to whom these phenomena may mean something, and who can be questioned about it or whose behaviour can be studied.

Summing up, we have come to the following results:

1) The primary concern of the phenomenological scholar is with the 'subjective' meaning of religious expressions and of religious phenomena, which he tries to understand;
2) The possibilities of his research depend, on one hand, on whether he deals only with phenomena, or also with direct expressions; and, on the other hand, on whether he investigates past-religion, or religion which is alive at the present time;
3) Most fruitful for meaning research is the study of living religion, where direct religious expressions are available;
4) In the process of understanding, there is a reconstruction or constitution of the background or universe, with regard to which meanings and intentions of the investigated expressions and phenomena can be brought to light.

At this point we may broach a question to which we shall return later: what might we understand, in this approach, by 'religion'? In our opinion, from a descriptive point of view, a particular religion might be con-

sidered to be a certain, often complicated system of meanings or significances, which have one or more or many symbols or reference points
to what might be called the transcendent sources of these meanings, or
better the 'intended object' of their intention(s). Of religion as such, in
this way, no definition can be given. We might say, however, that through
religious meaning man has a sense of a source of meaning, and that the
religious experience appears to bring about the 'rooting' of man in
meaningful reality.

Resuming briefly some points of the preceding argumentation we
come to the following conclusion with regard to 'understanding'.
Empirical research on all available materials is the *conditio sine qua non*
of any scholarly study of religion. During such research, when we want
to do justice to the materials studied, certain problems arise, which we
can identify as problems of meaning, more specifically: subjective meaning. In order to arrive at any understanding of religious phenomena which
goes beyond their factual classification, we have to view them as expressions of people and to search for the significance of such expressions
and phenomena for certain groups or persons. Any understanding of
such meanings which claims to be made on a scholarly level, should be
able to justify itself *rationally*. This in its turn implies a theory about the
phenomenon of religion, which must be developed by methodical reflection and has to be checked with the empirical data available.

Intentions. We saw that what we call the 'intention' helps us to understand the religious significance of something for someone, in so far as
this implies some kind of *tertium datum* or intended object to which an
explicit reference is made or a reference to which is implicitly present.
The particular feature of a religious significance appears thereby to be
that the intended object has some quality of absolute validity for the
person or community concerned, and that it is allowed to function
concretely as a first value in a symbolic belief, value and action system, a
value with a powerful appeal. If an analysis of the daily life world, without any religion, already shows certain cores of significance for the people
concerned which have a clearly symbolic function in the social sphere,
this is still much more the case if one analyses a religious life world.

A number of direct religious expressions can indeed successfully be interpreted in terms of intentions contained in such expressions. This holds true not only for the 'strong' expressions of religious meaning, as expressed in individual records of prayer and vision, of mystical experience and gnostic illumination, but also for those religious expressions which have at first sight a less strong meaning, as is the case with sacred stories including myths, sacred texts containing commands and prohibitions, with rituals and prescribed ways of behaving. In practice it will be more difficult here to reconstruct such intentions since they are less explicit and do not have the 'disturbing' quality of the strong expressions, but rather the character of founding regularity and allowing periodical renovation. A third category of phenomena has a decidedly weak expression of religious meaning. Often their meaning is implied but 'forgotten' by most people; these things are within the realm of custom or even folklore and their neglect does not necessarily lead to a crisis. But even apart from religion, on closer phenomenological analysis any human life world contains a network of intentions which move not only in various directions but also occur on different levels, conscious and unconscious. As said before, one of the main tasks of phenomenological research is to lay bare such basic intentions. In the last analysis they have to do with fundamental structures of human subjective and intersubjective existence, and a number of concrete expressions of man can be interpreted as to their subjective meaning by correlating them with such structures. Among these expressions, those deserve special attention through which certain basic intentions enunciate themselves about the fact of man's and the world's existence as such.

From at least three sides questions have been raised to which the concept of intention may help find an answer. First, structural research as carried out by C. Lévi-Strauss, convincingly shows certain formal relations between structural elements, according to patterns of signifying-signified. There is need now for a heuristic concept by means of which the contents, the 'material' side of such relations can be grasped. Second, any research on subjective meaning shows the need for research on the involvements and commitments of the person or community under consideration. The concept of 'intention' can have the heuristic function to investigate such a 'subjective' involvement or commitment with reference to what may be called an intended object as a *tertium datum*. And third, there is the question, formulated earlier, of how to relate the ideational contents of a phenomenon or a system to its appeal to certain persons or communities in certain conditions. Again, the concept of 'intention' would allow the analysis of such an appeal, providing the link between an ideology and the people living by it.

If the existence of intentions would be an appropriate hypothesis both to explain the meaning which a given object may acquire for a given subject and to investigate the realm of subjective meaning, how could such intentions be described and then defined?

Intentions could perhaps best be called potential movements into future directions into which man, individually or in community, either is going already or at least would want to go: directions which, in their turn, have immediate consequences for his present orientation. Intentions are not the result of rational thought only, and man's awareness of them, unless in sudden flashes of clarity of consciousness, is not immediate so that he must become aware of them through their symbolic expression. Persons and groups can themselves interpret, suppress or bely their intentions which may also become rationalized and subsequently changed. So intentions may manifest themselves in that particular sort of reflection which takes its departure either from a flash of consciousness or from a symbolic expression; the 'real' intention converts thereby into a 'reflected' intention.

Group intentions undergo changes according to time and place; the cultural context largely determines what intentions can legitimately occur in a given society and which ones have to be suppressed; it also determines the forms in which they can manifest themselves. All in all, intentions are vitally important for the understanding of human reality. Needless to say that they are not necessarily religious in themselves; they may get, however, a religious quality. This appears to depend on the quality of the intended object to which they are directed, and on the quality of man's relation to this intended object. Such a religious quality manifests itself through the absolute validity or the trans-empirical reference which makes itself felt to the people concerned, involved or committed.

On the occasion of certain events such intentions express themselves creatively in forms felt to be charged with meaning and becoming phenomena proper as 'significant facts'. When the meaning of such a phenomenon, in the culture concerned, is felt to have a religious quality, we are allowed to speak of a 'religious phenomenon'. And just as phenomena in general, themselves expressions of intentions, may awaken intentions among people who have to do with them, so religious phenomena in their turn may awaken similar or new intentions among those who perceive them.

Intentional research. The study of subjective meaning in religion would consequently consist, to an appreciable extent, in the analysis of religious expressions and phenomena as to their intentions. Just as culture implies some surplus meaning of art and religion, play and intersubjectivity, which show intentions within and beyond the need of sheer organic survival, religion would give some absolute justification, foundation or at least validity to certain aspects of that culture. Like other meanings, the forms of awareness which have to do with ultimate sense and nonsense become intelligible in the light of intentions which phenomenological research is able to lay bare. As mentioned earlier, this requires on the part of the student an elaborate knowledge of the factual total context within which such meanings occur. It then requires the analysis of a set of coherent expressions, whatever may be their ways and forms, as to their intentions. In order to be able to distinguish such intentions, the student must develop a kind of 'feeling' for the 'intended objects' to which these intentions refer, through a thorough acquaintance with the ideals and strivings, illusions and frustrations, as these are expressed in his materials. Next, the student has to check and verify his reconstruction or constitution of what functioned as subjective meaning at a given place and time, by means of his empirical data and through logical reflection and control.

Such an intentional research, to be sure, comes down to a fundamentally new style phenomenology of religion which distinguishes itself basically from what we called the 'classical' phenomenology of religion. The following key concepts would be of use, provided that their meaning be defined in a lucid way. The *epoche* would be the suspension or bracketing of the natural world of the student, his openness for the essential problems proper to human existence, and his focussing on the specific object of his interest and investigation. The quest for what is *essential* would be basically a problem of significance or meaning. If religious data are understood as expressing, among other things, a 'religious' meaning, a proper distinction should be made between direct 'expressions' on one hand, and transmitted expressions or 'phenomena' proper on the other hand. With regard to the direct expressions the search would be for what has given rise to such an expression and for its specific content. With regard to the transmitted expressions the search would be for what has been or is their significance to different people at different times and places, as a range of meanings within a formal structure.

Intentionality would be understood as the very fact of the existence and functioning of intentions as a fundamental feature of all human reality. In order to be able to come to any valid interpretation of intentions, the phenomenological analyst, parallel to the psychoanalyst in his particular field, will have to go through a process of catharsis in order to arrive himself at a level of intentionality as such. He will be attentive then not only to the existing cultural forms which allow of certain religious expressions, but also to those mechanisms of repression at play within each society with regard to deviant or at least diverging intentions wanting to express themselves, against those intentions which are generally admitted. In this way, phenomenological research could be called a 'psychoanalysis' of cultural and religious expressions, in terms of man's identionality. An important element in any such a phenomenological analysis is the distinction between different *layers of significance* in which the expression is imbedded. If, in the case of a religious phenomenon, one of these layers is what may be called that of its 'religious' significance or meaning, a rigorous methodical distinction has to be made between that religious significance that the phenomenon has to given people in a given culture, and the religious meaning which the student himself, on the basis of his experience, might be inclined to attribute to that phenomenon.

This type of research with regard to subjective meaning can be carried out, in principle, as well by those who investigate the phenomenon as outsiders to the tradition within which it occurs, as by those who have been involved in that particular religious tradition: on condition that the same objectification process is carried out by both types of students. In a parallel way, the conclusions both of religiously-committed and of not-religiously-committed students, in so far as both have gone through the same objectification process, should be taken into account. Characteristically, intentional research, if carried out correctly, will be able not only to see different shades of significance — religious and otherwise — in one and the same 'religious' phenomenon, but also to distinguish such 'meanings' from each other, so that one and the same phenomenon can be seen from different sides or aspects. On the other hand, a comparative study can be made of the different expressions which certain human existential data or problems have found in different cultures and their religions, and of the various solutions which were proposed according to different intentions realized in these cultures.

Religion as signification system. Finally we want to summarize the relevance of the preceding pages for the study of religion as meaning: religions can be considered and studied as signification systems.

We said earlier that within a culture something appears to be 'religious' when one or more cores of significance designate something that has absolute validity for the person or group concerned and that is transcendent to empirical reality. It is the fact of something signifying some other reality, which may lead to religion. Accordingly, a religion can be viewed as a great signification system, and thus as a system whereby a number of people can find potential meaning. This happens through specific cores of significance through which specific intentions are awakened and directed toward an 'intended object' which in religion is source of significance.

It is in this way, for instance, that we are able to understand structures of those religions which stretch beyond one particular group or culture. Through their specific cores of significance they provide a world of discourse, a space of speech beyond the given local cultures, which makes possible to the people concerned a common discourse on the basis of what are held to be common evidences or implicit self-evidences, thanks to the common recognition of an 'intended object' as supreme truth and value. And it seems to be through the communication of appeals or messages via the 'symbolic' cores of significance that the people concerned can communicate with reality and with each other, and that a religion may be said to be a communication system as well as a signification system.

The concrete functioning of religion as a signification system, and specifically as a system which offers meaning, seems to be possible within a given culture only through an institutionalization which allows certain well-determined reference-channels for transcendent, or 'founding' meaning. Consequently, in the course of a religion's history a process of institutionalization and de-institutionalization goes on, parallel to and in an inner tension with the emerging or weakening intentions of persons and groups, which tension provides for continuing development.

Within each given religion or religious world, certain phenomena occur as charged with religious significance, while others do not: there is within each religious world, religion and culture, a certain specificity in the way in which certain religious phenomena occur while others do not, and in the way in which they are interrelated. In the same way there are in each culture specific connections between certain religious and given socio-cultural structures. In a phenomenological perspective, this has to do with the meanings which, within a given culture, can be given to life and world, be it less on a personal than on a communal level.

Beyond such specific religious structures and meanings, there also appear to be more general and basic structures of human religiosity, respectively a-religiosity; they make intelligible, among other things, transitions from religious to non-religious meanings, and vice versa. On closer consideration, each religious significance appears to give rise to a differentiation on the part of the receivers, varying from recognition to negation, through simple withdrawal or making an active use of it for other than 'religious' purposes, that is by manipulating it. At the basis of a particular religion as a signification system there appear to be certain specific problems for which it tries to provide a solution, be it on another level than that of empirical reality. A religious meaning, consequently, could very well be interpreted as the solution for a specific problem or set of problems, be it a solution provided by an 'intentional' view, on a more or less 'sublimated' level, with the awareness of a possible ultimate sense of life and reality. In this way, religious significances and meanings have an anthropological dimension, with intentionality as a basic characteristic of human reality. Concretely, this would imply that the phenomenological analyst, in order to understand the appeal or 'message' of a religious meaning to a particular person or community, will have to reconstruct the underlying problem to which this meaning provides a kind of solution. The question whether such a 'religious' solution is adequate in given circumstances is beyond his judgement.

If it is true that the student of religion is professionally working on what, at least to the people concerned, are no more than the remainings, the sediments — or at best: the objective expressions — of religious expressions, and if it is true that he studies them as facts in themselves and not necessarily as forms of human expression, two alternative approaches present themselves for meaning research. One approach is to try to demonstrate a rational meaning throughout these facts, correlate with a particular theory of religion and culture. The other approach assumes, focussing on 'subjective' religious meaning, that both the intelligibility of religious expressions and that of religion as a signification system is maximal if we take our departure in research on human intentions. In both approaches, there is a direct relationship between the way in which concrete religious facts are interpreted and the way in which reflection on the phenomenon of religion takes place.

In the second approach, a systematically working intentional research is concerned with the various designs or projects which man, as a member of a community and as an individual, has given and gives to his existence in this world and beyond, from the needs for survival onwards. Such designs are held to express intentions which are basically answers to existential problems with which mankind has been confronted. In this approach there is a stress on logic, a definite refusal of irrationalism: intentional research is based on its own reflected reasonability with regard to meaningful facts. The student will have to resist the old temptation to create a world apart from the real world, in this case to carry out an ideation for its own sake. His sole concern is to X-ray the real world of man on its intentionalities: religion is not to be reduced to some kind of ideal reality, but is here interpreted in terms of human reality, as ideality itself is understood in terms of human existence.

In a way, it is legitimate to say that man is always forced to realize and appreciate how his fellow-men speak and behave. In the study of religion this necessity is, so to say, professionalized, and the student of religion inquires specifically how others have put ultimate questions and tried to arrive at solutions for them in the form of religious meanings. So the student of this discipline has, in his field of research, the absolute everywhere around: yet, as a student, he has himself to work without absolutes. His concern is the man for whom something appears to have an absolute quality, not the absolute itself.

Intentional research is a technique to grasp, at least approximately, meanings of expressions or significances of phenomena for people. And just as we can approach the phenomenon of religion now in a way different from a hundred or fifty years ago, we equally do this with regard to meaning and significance. This has to do in part with new ways in which something is felt to be 'religious' or 'meaningful'; in any case, not only the problem of religion but also that of meaning has to be completely reformulated. It also has to do in part with a development of our notion of rationality in the discipline. Against an older rationalistic climate there came an anti-rationalistic reaction stressing the irrational both in religion and in semantics. At present logic claims its dues again, and we have come to the point that we can speak of the 'logic' of myths and symbols, and of 'fields' of intelligibility so that an intelligence entering into a new field is able to conclude to a series of evidences which have their own logic in this field. The reformulation of the problem of religion and meaning may have to do in part also with a development of the notion of 'the other' in present-day thought. Especially in phenomenology there must be signalized a growing concern with the category of the other, with questions like: what the other means with his expressions, what something means to the other, what place to give him, how to relate to him, etc. Such questions are, indirectly, of fundamental importance for the interpretation of religious expressions and phenomena emanating from 'the other' with regard to whom the student somehow takes a stand. Two extreme attitudes may usefully be recalled here: on one hand the consideration of religious data as objects in themselves, not to be interpreted in terms of any human dimension or reference; and on the other hand the consideration of religious data as testimonies of a religious faith of people with whom one wants to identify one self. Unfortunately, these attitudes were often connected with the absurd alternative of being either 'against' or 'for' religion in the study of religion itself.

Evidently a hermeneutics of subjective religious meaning, as sketched in the above leads to an interpretation of religious data in terms of human existence. Its starting-point is that man meets reality and confronts problems which are given with his environment and with his own nature. Our hypothesis is that situations and problems are digested by man in many ways, as viewed from his basic intentions; this 'digestion' could result in solutions which have some definite, absolute quality for those concerned, and which express themselves on the level of 'religious' meanings of which mankind's religious past bears evidence in a long record of religious expressions. The phenomenological analyst, using those data which have a clear ideational content and about which sufficient other data are available, tries to uncover their subjective meaning by questioning and interrogating the material on certain basic questions which may open up the implied intentions. Religion, in this way, is studied as a self-expression of human existence in different cultures and circumstances of place and time. Structure and meaning of human expressions, including the religious ones, are related to the very core of human existence: its intentionality. And if religion cannot be studied directly as existential reality, at least its expressions can be interpreted as to their subjective meaning in the light of human intentions: in so far as the materials allow us to uncover them.

Religion understood as meaning is, seen in this light, a human expression with an intentional core, an existential component, within a social reality. By putting the right questions in his dialogue with the materials before him, the student of religion is able, in principle, to come to valid conclusions notably concerning man's dealing with his existence. Like art and play, religion is to be understood as a real human expression: no need to make a myth, an ideology or a 'religion' about it. Our field of research — subjective meaning — is the human variable of self-interpretations and testimonies against the constancy of man's sheer existence on earth.

The author is aware of the *exploratory* nature of the present paper in which an attempt is made to investigate the possibility of *research on subjectivity and meaning* in the field of religion and of human expressions in general. He wants to express his sincere gratitude to Professor R.L.Nettler, of Carleton University, Ottawa, who kindly corrected the English style of this paper.

Religious Ethology
Some Methodological Aspects

0.0. INTRODUCTION

Since 1961 the Institute or Religious Iconography of the State University of Groningen has been collecting pictorial material of various kinds for the study of religions. This archaeological, iconographical and ethnographical material, consisting of slides and photographs, is given basic documentation according to a standard list, and then provided with fuller scientific documentation. The stock is listed under the headings: sculpture, masks, paintings, reliefs and carvings, architecture, objects of ordinary use, man in his milieu, and until recently it also comprised a large quantity of heterogeneous material preresenting people in more or less clear situations of religious relevance. The necessity of correlating the divisions named above and making it possible to establish a serviceable system of cross-reference, led to theoretical reflection and more especially to seeking a possibility of making the theory formation of science of religion, of which this volume offers an impression, operational for designing taxonomies and classificatory systems in science of religion.

0.1. *The Methodic Primacy of Behaviour*

The first consequence was to make a heading '(religious) behaviour' as matrix and point of departure for cross-references for the whole systematic documentation. This methodic primacy of behaviour for research and classification is based initially upon the simple fact that no serviceable system of cross-reference can be devised based on one of the other headings, since these all contain elements of material culture or artifacts; at the same time the *methodic primacy of behaviour* may be posited from the hypothesis that religion as a cultural institution is best approached and analysed through the behavioural aspects. In the words of Spiro:

... In short, the existence of a sociocultural variable (here: religion, A.V.) means that in any sense of 'behavior' — cognitive, affective, or motor — there occurs some behavior in which, or by which, the variable in question is instanced. Hence, a theory of the 'existence' of religion must ultimately be capable of explaining religious 'behavior' (Spiro, 1966: 99).

Spiro's definition of religion also stresses the behavioural aspects:

... religion (is) an institution consisting of culturally patterned *interaction* with culturally postulated superhuman beings' (*ibid.*: 96).

This interaction may be direct or intermediate; the latter category, which Nadel calls 'co-activity' (Nadel, 1951: 28), also includes 'norms, beliefs, in short, ideological elements'. For

... an idea not communicated is beyond examination ... Nor can symbols of whatever kind ... ever be imagined away from the interplay of behavior; for they are both the product of action and the starting points of new action, on the part of those who perceive and comprehend the symbol ...' (*ibid.*: 28-29).

Spiro too has clearly shown that what we call 'culture' is an abstraction of the observed behaviours in common of many individuals in a specified group (while that which we call 'personality' is equally an abstraction of human behaviour, viz. that of the individual) (cf. Spiro, 1951). The concrete empirical source of hese abstractions is the same, it is the mutually patterned and resonant behaviour of human beings in society (cf. La Barre, 1970: 46-47).

0.2. *Culture and Behaviour*

The forms of behaviour which constitute the principal subject-matter of anthropological research, should according to Nadel be 'recurrent, regular, coherent and predictable':

... the subject matter of our inquiry is standardized behaviour patterns: their integrated totality is culture' (Nadel, 1951: 28-29).

I do not agree, though, with Leertouwer's view that unique, unpredictable, irregular and incoherent actions may very well have meaning in a metaphysical sense, but not in terms of cultural science (Leertouwer,

1973: 10); it should at least be attempted to relate such behaviour to—, or to set it against the background of —, some established standardized pattern (cf. Nadel, 1951: 30). And even if this does not prove possible and analysis of such behaviour has to be left to other disciplines, this does not imply that the behaviour in question is idiosyncratic in terms of the cultural sciences.

For a fuller discussion of the relation between culture and behaviour, methodically and theoretically considered (cf. Tennekes, 1971: 80f.). Here I will only quote a few sentences of immediate relevance to the present argument:

... I stress that in one way or another, the cultural anthropologist deals with behavior ... (*ibid.*: 80),

and this behavior as object of culturological research includes both the 'pattern for behavior' ('normative behavior patterns') and the 'pattern of behavior' ('factual behavior patterns'). (cf. *ibid.*: 85).

... Just as 'social structure', so also does 'culture' presuppose concrete, acting persons; one can no more separate a system of symbolic meanings from concrete people as one can a system of social relationships and interactions. (*ibid.*: 82).

... It is not really correct to say that 'everything that man does' IS culture ... It is better to say that all this may be viewed as culture ... I would indeed describe behavior as 'the things people have, the things they do and what they think.' This is a broader definition than usual in cultural anthropology. But to me behavior has both an 'inner' and an 'outer' aspect. To 'inner' behavior belong those matters which are not immediately visible, such as attitudes, convictions, ideas, etc.; and among 'outer' behavior I include artifacts in which human behavior has, as it were, crystallized or hardened: houses, tools, works of art, etc. (*ibid.*: 84).

I believe one could hardly imagine a more apt and far-reaching description of the theoretical and methodical primacy of behaviour, in this case religious behaviour, as the starting-point for the analysis and classification of material and immaterial elements of the cultural institution called 'religion'.

0.3 *Starting-points for a Taxonomy of Behaviour*

In projecting criteria for a taxonomy of behaviour, we must take account of both aspects named above, the 'inner' and the 'outer' aspect. It seems to me that we could use, also for the classifying of religious cultural elements, the list of 7 major facets employed by Murdock and others as primary basis of classification:

1. Every element of culture involves ... *a patterned activity*, i.e., a customary norm of motor, verbal, or implicit (covert or ideational) behavior;

2. ... an activity is normally considered appropriate only under *certain circumstances*, e.g., of time or place;

3. ... customary activities are frequently associated with a *particular subject*, i.e., a culturally defined class of persons, the occupants of a particular status, or the members of a specified social group;

4. ... an activity is commonly directed toward *some object*, which may be an inanimate thing, an animal, or a person (or, a superhuman being; A.V.);

5. ... many activities are accomplished by the use of some *means* external to both the subject and the object;

6. ... activities are normally performed with a *purpose* or goal in mind;

7. ... an activity commonly has some concrete *result*, affecting either the subject, the object, or both. (Murdock a.o., 1967: XXI-XXII).

The facets named under 2 to 7 inclusive offer few methodological problems. With no. 1 it is otherwise. How for instance can uncustomary, idiosyncratic, but religiously relevant behaviour be classified? Moreover, simple classification is only one of the different ways of perceiving order in the phenomena; besides the *classificatory sense* we must distinguish a *systematic sense*: the former concerns 'a relation of similarity contrasting them with all other phenomena', the latter 'structural-functional relations' (McKinney, 1969: 8-9).

These two different modes of cognitively ordering phenomena are combined in a typology — for this is built up of types — of which the double theoretical function is implicit: to classify and to systematize. The question is whether through the process of conceptualization, generalization and reduction, — and typification is a component part of this process — a typology of religious behaviour can be designed capable of serving as a heuristic device in the analysis and classification of e.g. a collection of pictorial material. To this problem I shall return later on in this paper.

1.0. RELIGION IS A CULTURAL INSTITUTION

That religion is a cultural institution is a truism which can only be ignored in the field of metaphysics. However:

... This means that the variables constituting a religious system have the same ontological status as those of other cultural systems: its beliefs are normative, its rituals collective, its values prescriptive ... Religion has the same methodological status as other cultural systems, i.e., religious variables are to be explained by the same explanatory schemata — historical, structural, functional, and causal — as those by which other cultural variables are explained (Spiro, 1966: 97).

The taking up of this position has some methodological consequences: the last quotation emphasizes Drijvers's remark that the primacy of theory is not substantial but only operational (1973: 58).

The question now arises, what results the various anthropological approaches to religion have produced (cf. Van Baal, 1971), and whether these results can be correlated in some way. That is to say, there is a growing need for a macro-theoretical framework as operational point of departure for applying the various strategies of research and as frame of correlation for combining the results obtained.

We shall return below to this possible macro-theoretical framework. First we must say a few words regarding concepts such as 'culture', 'cultural institution', 'cultural system', etc.

1.1. *The Culture Concept*

A critical survey of the numerous definitions and descriptions of 'Culture' is superfluous here (cf. Kroeber and Kluckhohn, 1952). Suitable for further use are, I think, the descriptions of Van Doorn and Lammers:

... the totality of what man has acquired, which is shared by a number of persons and which can be transmitted to others. Culture ... is the total result of man's power of objectification. It is his design of reality (1967: 21).

This is in essential agreement with the formulation of Tennekes:

... Culture is a system of symbolic meanings which supply man with his orientation to reality (that is, to his natural environment, to his relations with his fellowmen, and to himself (1971: 61).

... it is ... the totality of aims, etc., which determine actual behavior (*ibid.*: 82).

Geertz also formulates his culture concept in terms of the same purport:

... an historically transmitted pattern of meanings embodied in symbols, a system of inherited conceptions expressed in symbolic forms by means of which men communicate, perpetuate and develop their knowledge about and attitudes toward life (Geertz, 1966: 3).

The common aspects of all cultures are expressed by Murdock in a series of seven basic assumptions: culture is learned, is inculcated, is social, is ideational, is gratifying, is adaptive, is interpretative (cf. Murdock, 1940: 361-370). It seems to me that these basic assumptions can form a serviceable set of co-ordinates for the analysis of the cultural system 'religion' (cf., e.g., Spiro, 1966).

1.2. *Socio-cultural Systems*

Nadel's definition of culture, which fits in so well with my line of thought, was already cited above: 'the integrated totality of standardized behavior patterns' (1951: 29). This conception of culture, inclusive as it is, only covers part of the reality which requires to be placed in a macro-theory for anthropological research. This reality may be summarized in the term '*socio-cultural systems*', the two components of which are described by Nadel as follows:

... Society, as I see it, means the totality of social facts projected on to the dimension of relationships and groupings; culture, the same totality in the dimension of action (*ibid.*: 79, 80),

that is, 'action in the wider sense, with its three co-ordinates language, idea systems, and physical action' (*ibid.*: 85). When further references are made in this paper to 'socio-cultural systems', this two-dimensional model may be borne in mind.

1.3. *Institutions*

'... The term institution, in fact, is so variously used that it is doubtful if it has a single meaning common to all its applications' said L. T. Hob-house (in: Nadel, 1951: 108n.); but all the same it is possible to give a functional definition of the concept. The principal aspects of institutions are, according to Becker-Wiese: the conceptual character, that lies in the function or purpose the researcher ascribes to them; the means available for the realization of the concept; and the normative character of the whole (*ibid.*).

Radcliffe-Brown defines institutions as 'standardized modes of be-haviour' (*ibid.*: 109), which is close to Nadel's view:

... By institution, then, we shall mean a standardized mode of social behaviour or, since social behaviour means co-activity, a standardized mode of co-activity (*ibid.* 108).

(for the concept 'co-activity' see under 0.1.)
The most important facets of this definition are in Nadel's formulation:
1. The degree and nature of the standardization visible in the co-activity;
2. The group of individuals or the 'personnel' who are its carriers;
3. The purposive orientation, the aim-contents, of the activity.
Moreover,

... we should also include data which ... represent prerequisite conditions, namely, the physical environment in which, and the material tools with which, any institution is realised (*ibid.*: 111).

These facets constitute in my opinion the analytical components for religion as a 'cultural institution', which as such is only to be distinguished from other cultural institutions 'by virtue of its reference to superhuman beings', and like all other institutions may be subdivided into 'belief, value and action systems'. (Spiro, 1966: 98).

2.0. PHENOMENOLOGICAL AND ANTHROPOLOGICAL APPROACHES

Up to the present it is still the phenomenological method, characterized as systematic or comparative science of religion, from which researchers are generally wont to equip themselves for the examination of 'religion'.

For a critical evaluation of this method I may refer to the papers of Van Baaren and Leertouwer, in which the latter justly remarks that the phenomenological method prevents Van der Leeuw and Widengren from doing justice to religious behaviour as a comparatively independent category of phenomena. The methodic primacy of behaviour (religious behaviour) I have postulated, requires other, anthropological approaches — at least in so far as the subject is suited to them.

Geertz is fairly pessimistic regarding the results so far obtained by anthropological work on religion; in his opinion we see 'the anthropological study of religion ... in fact in a state of general stagnation; it is living off the conceptual capital of its ancestors, Durkheim, Weber, Freud, or Malinowksi'. If research tries to rise above this academic level, there is risk of 'arbitrary eclecticism, superficial theory-mongering and sheer intellectual confusion'. That the present paper has not escaped these faults must be at once admitted but, to speak with Geertz, 'I, at least, can see no other road of escape from ... the dead hand of competence' (Geertz, 1966: passim).

2.1. Theory and Macro-theory

The principal anthropological theories — structuralism, functionalism, culture-and-personality, historical particularism, statistical methods and so on — have each to some extent contributed to insight in causes and functions of religious systems. Methodically considered, however, the results of these various approaches are heterogeneous and will not fit into a coherent relation. Now a 'holistic meta-theory' seems to me a (tempting) fiction, yet there is great need of a *macro- theory*, based on *nomothetic principles*, as framework in which the various methodic approaches, while maintaining their own methodological presuppositions, may be profitably combined. The relation between the various 'general theories' and a 'macro-theory' is represented in the schema given below (adapted from Pelto, 1970: 3). The various methodological procedures, each comprising the totality of analytical operations between 'the real world of things and events' and 'general theory and models, etc.', must be related to each other on the basis of the propositions and hypotheses of a macro-theory.

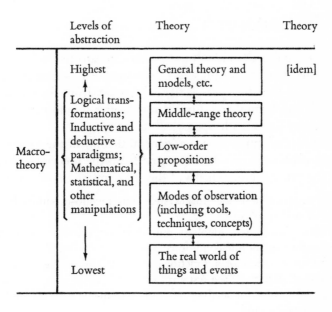

2.2. Is it possible to construct such a macro-theoretical framework in which the various theoretical approaches to cultural institutions, e.g. religion, may be profitably related to each other? Activated in part by need for classificatory systems for the documentation of religious iconography, I have postulated that from the point of view of method the analysis and classification of behaviour comes first; this position finds support in the methodological propositions of various anthropologists (see above). It seems to me this primacy of behaviour should also be the *Leitmotiv* in designing a macro-theory.

An exposition of the basic principles for such a theory I have taken mainly from Marvin Harris's *The Rise of Anthropological Theory* (1968), while account must be taken of what was said above regarding behaviour and culture. For, according to Pelto, 'Harris ... insists that he is studying culture, though his goals are clearly the description of behavior patterns, based largely on nonverbal data. In this view, verbal materials are of some use in understanding and classifying human behavior, but they are distinctly secondary' (Pelto, 1970: 82).

3.0. OF ALL PEOPLE: MARX

The study of 'culture' and 'cultural systems' means that rules, or if preferred 'regularities' are formulated in synchronous — functional — and diachronous — causal — perspective; this arises from the consideration that to seek and formulate historical regularities should have methodological priority in the anthropological sciences.

The first formulations of such a 'general theory' in the form of a 'law of cultural evolution' may be abstracted from the theories of Marx and Engels. The principal ingredients of this 'law' are:

1. ...the trisection of sociocultural systems into techno-economic base, social organization, and ideology;

2. ... the explanation of ideology and social organization as adaptive responses to techno-economic conditions;

3. ... the formulation of a functionalist model providing for interactive aspects between all parts of the system;

4. ... the provision for analysis of both system-maintaining and system-destroying variables; and

5. ... the pre-eminence of culture over race.

(Harris, 1968: 240).

This 'strategy of cultural materialism' starts from the assumption that '... the explanation for cultural differences and similarities is to be found in the techno-economic processes responsible for the production of the material requirements of biosocial survival', and that '... the techno-economic parameters (i.e., characteristic elements or constant factors; A.V.) of sociocultural systems exert selective pressures in favor of certain types of organizational structures and upon the survival and spread of definite types of ideological complexes' (Harris, 1968: 241). (N.B. It is therefore possible to apply the research strategy of Marx without taking over his specific analyses of e.g. capitalistic structures of society!).

The importance of this theory for designing a 'general law of evolution' is that '... the most powerful generalizations about history are to be found by studying the relationship between the qualitative and quantitative aspects of culture energy systems as the independent variables and the quantitative and qualitative aspects of the other domains of sociocultural phenomena as the dependent ones' (ibid.: 651).

The essence of cultural materialism is that it

... directs attention to the *interaction* between behavior and environment as mediated by the human organism and its cultural apparatus. It does so as an order of priority in conformity with the prediction that group structure and ideology are responsive to these classes of material conditions,

taking its departure therefore from the proposition that

... social organization and ideology tend to be the *dependent variables* in any large diachronic sample of sociocultural systems (*ibid.*: 658-659).

As macro-theory of sociocultural evolution, cultural materialism (i.e., the principle of techno-economic and techno-environmental determinism) is analogous with Darwin's doctrine of natural selection. As the latter gives priority to the study of differential reproductive success, thus the principle of techno-environmental, techno-economic determinism gives priority to the study of the material circumstances of sociocultural life:

... this principle holds that similar technologies applied to similar environments tend to produce similar arrangements of labor in production and distribution, and that these in turn call forth similar kinds of social groupings, which justify and coördinate their activities by means of similar systems of values and beliefs (*ibid.*: 4);

or, in a present-day anthropological formulation:

... it is the techno-environmental and techno-economic conditions in which the human population finds itself with demand priority of analysis because there exists overwhelming evidence that these are the parts of the total sociocultural system which in the long run and in most cases swing social structure and ideology into functional conformity (*ibid.*: 566).

3.1. It is not superfluous here to point out a frequent misunderstanding. Often it is objected to the cultural materialist research strategy sketched above, that it is one-sided and that economic explanations are 'single-factor' explanations and therefore simplistic. It is supposed to be equivalent to economic determinism, only recognizing man's rational aspects since the irrational aspects are either superfluous or at any rate dysfunctional.

Such reproach stems from anti-economic-determinist dogmatism or from ignorance regarding the macro-theoretical character of cultural materialism, as this only utilizes the techno-economic and techno-environmental parameters of sociocultural systems as independent variables. Moreover, it is exactly this approach which is able to place apparently irrational or dysfunctional aspects in a causal-functional relation. That even a wide, but superficial interest in economic phenomena is not sufficient to make this causal-functional connexion, is shown by Malinowski's analysis of the Kula ring. In his Preface to 'Argonauts of the Western Pacific', Frazer does indeed praise Malinowski's stressing of economic factors, yet it is precisely the motivations and sentiments arising from *non-economic needs* which dominate the entire Kula, according to Malinowski's description. The complex functions of such systems only become clear if one begins with the cultural-materialist proposition that the social and ideological variables are dependent on the techno-economic and techno-environmental ones, and then in this framework proceeds to order the relevant ecological, economic, political, demographic, cognitive and other data and to formulate hypotheses. Truly no field for oversimplification!

3.2. The Search for Laws in History

The great importance of cultural materialism lies in the nomothetic character of this theory, which seeks for the regularities in the developments of sociocultural systems. This also was, and in certain respects still is, the aim of *statistical cross-cultural surveys* (Tylor, Spencer, Steinmetz, Hobhouse, Wheeler, Ginsberg, Murdock *et al.*). However,

... statistics cannot validate functional hypotheses or hypotheses about origins when the data are synchronic.' (Jorgensen, 1966: 162, in Harris, 1968: 618).
... one glaring defect ... is characteristic of all the statistical comparative studies carried out since Tylor's pioneering essay. None of them have been capable of showing causal relations ... None of the studies have concerned themselves with time-structured data ... (Harris, 1968: 618).

and:

... statistical results can never be better than the ethnografical data (Driver and Kroeber, 1932: 255).

All the same statistical data can and must be used to supplement other approaches. Particularly the 'Human Relations Area Files', the 'World

Ethnografic Sample', the 'Outline of Cultural Materials' of Murdock a.o. are very useful, sometimes even indispensable, yet the unavoidable conclusion remains 'that there is no substitute for macro-theory founded on detailed diachronic and synchronic causal-functional analysis of specific cases' (Harris, 1968: 633). (Cf. also: A. J. Köbben, 'New Ways of Presenting an Old Idea: The Statistical Method in Social Anthropology', 1952).

For an extensive review of the contributions made by the various anthropological theories to the setting up of an operational *cultural materialist research strategy*, and of the feedback of this strategy to those theories, see the book by Harris. It is not surprising that especially archeology has had good results from this approach.

Finally, if anthropology is to be a science of history, then it cannot be sufficiently stressed that

... the vindication of the strategy of cultural materialism ... lies in the capacity ... to generate major explanatory hypotheses which can be subjected to the tests of ethnographic and archaeological research, modified if necessary, and made part of a corpus of theory equally capable of explaining the most generalised features of universal history and the most exotic specialties of particular cultures (Harris, 1968: 687).

4.0. PROBLEMS OF OPERATIONALIZATION

The discussion as to whether operational concepts for the description and analysis of behaviour, conceptions etc. should be taken from the cognitive system of the actor or from the scientific conceptual apparatus of the researcher, is usually conducted in terms of the 'emic-etic' dichotomy. (Terms introduced by Kenneth Pike, on the analogy of the linguistic terms 'phonemic' and 'phonetic' (Pike 1954). Harris defines these terms as follows:

... emic statements refer to logico-empirical systems whose phenomenal distinctions or 'things' are built up out of contrasts and discriminations significant, meaningful, real, accurate, or in some other fashion regarded as appropriate by the actors themselves (Harris, 1968: 571).

... etic statements depend upon phenomenal distinctions judged appropriate by the community of scientific observers (*ibid.*: 575).

Thus the answer to the question whether certain concepts are emic or etic lies in their logico-empirical relation with cognitive processes. The language of anthropology consists of concepts resulting from a mixture of emic and etic operations. Naturally this distinction between *emic and etic* does not coincide with the contrast between *ideal and actual behaviour*. The latter contrast rests upon the consideration that '... there is one set of patterned regularities consisting of what people say or believe about what they do or should do and another set of patterned regularities concerned with what they "actually do".' The emic-etic dichotomy on the other hand,

... rests upon the epistemological significance of describing cultural things through categories and relations which are necessarily isomorphic with those appropriate or meaningful to the actors, as opposed to categories and relations which arise independently in the ethnographer's data language. Thus, actual behavior can be treated in both an emic and an etic fashion (*ibid.*: 580).

Obviously cross-cultural comparison of cultural concepts is only possible in etic categories.

4.1. We cannot enter into the complex problematic of cross-cultural comparison touched upon here; see for this matter *int. al.* Frank Moore (ed.): *Readings in Cross-Cultural Methodology*, 1961. Let me quote, however, a few remarks directly relevant to this argumentation:

... valid cross-cultural comparison could best proceed from the invariant points of reference supplied by the biological, psychological, and sociositua-tional 'givens' of human life;

for

... all cultures constitute so many somewhat distinct answers to essentially the same questions posed by human biology and by the generalities of the human situation (Kluckhohn, 1953, in Moore, 1961: 105),

a starting-point entirely in keeping with the cultural materialist research strategy.

... in any case, the crucial point is this: biological, psychological, and socio-situational universals afford the possibility of comparison of cultures in terms which are not ethnocentric, which depart from 'givens', begging no needless questions (Kluckhohn, 1953, in Moore, 1961: 101).

4.2. *Deductive Elements and Explanatory Schemata*

The methodic primacy of *behaviour*, within the framework of the *cultural-materialist research strategy* having biological, psychological and socio-situational *cultural universals* as invariant points of reference, on which basis *cross-cultural comparison* is possible: this is the deductive dimension for the research procedure. For the developing of operational (=intersubjectively meaningful) *explanatory schemata* aiming at the analysis of religion as a cultural institution, Spiro's article (1966) seems very important to me. His definition of religion as 'an institution consisting of culturally patterned interaction with culturally postulated superhuman beings' incorporates the chief deductive elements; it clearly delimits religion as a cultural institution from other cultural institutions by positing superhuman beings as the specific core variable; his systematic differentiation of religion in belief, value and action systems offers a very useful analytical model for correlation with other cultural systems. He combines the various approaches into two groups: causal and functional, both taking their departure from the aforesaid invariant points of reference, which constitute the needs for the 'satisfaction of which the religion is a vast instrumental reality.' Religious behaviour is thus motivated by '... the expectation of satisfying cognitive, substantive, and expressive desires; the corresponding functions can be called adjustive, adaptive and integrative' (Spiro, 1966: passim).

In his article Spiro does not discuss the problem of the origins of religion, since he considers speculations on this subject cannot be tested. We find a fascinating attempt at giving some theoretical support precisely to these untestable speculations in Weston La Barre's book: *The Ghost Dance; The Origins of Religion*. His psycho-cultural analyses of the causes and functions of religion fall entirely within the framework of cultural materialism as macro-theory; and on the basis of the presuppositions of this macro-theory, we see that Spiro's more functionalistic approach and La Barre's which is more causally oriented may be brought into fruitful relation.

Definite practical results have been obtained by this research strategy in the study of the Potlatch systems of the American Northwest Coast by Andrew Vayda and Wayne Suttles (cf. Harris, 1968: 311). This new approach also stresses the importance of the prestige accruing to the potlatch leaders from giving presents, food and other valuables, to members of other groups; but

... whereas this prestige has nothing but a completely inexplicable and unqualified penchant for self-glorification at its base in Benedict's account (1959), we now see that the entire prestige system was probably in definite and controlled articulation with aboriginal techno-environmental and techno-economic conditions vital to the maintenance of individual and collective life ...
... under aboriginal conditions, the Kwakiutl potlatch must have been one of the varieties of redistributive systems by which incipiently stratified social systems maintained their productivity levels and maximized their social cohesion (Harris, 1968: 313).

An explanatory scheme which is clearly very serviceable in the setting of the macro-theory described, is the so-called 'field-theory'. Leertouwer gives an example of its application in his paper (1973: 79ff.). Yinger renders 'the field context of religion' in the following model (1970: 89):

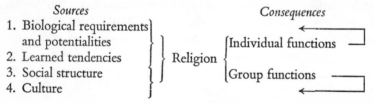

Yinger describes the advantages of a field-theoretical approach as follows:

... it more readily combines attention to individual and group elements, to part-whole relationships; ... Because in field theory individual and situation cannot even be defined fully, independently of each other, there is no chance that their mutual influences will be disregarded.
... a field approach can use both one-directional and feedback causal models ...
... a field approach makes no assumptions about system normalcy, and is as prepared to study the effects of disjunctions among the influences of the social structure, culture, and character as it is to study the effects of their conjunction ... (ibid.: 90).

5.1. Typology and Classification of Religious Behaviour

After consideration of the above, I would briefly return to my point of departure: the search for possibilities of constructing classification systems for scientific religious iconography.

To make my meaning clear: by '*taxonomy*' I understand 'the study of the general principles of a scientific (etic) classification'; by '*classification*', 'the systematic arrangement in groups or categories according to established criteria', these criteria being derived from the taxonomy; and by '*typology*', 'a classification based on types'.

In designing a typology of religious behaviour we are confronted with the same problematic that was discussed under 4.0. in the terminology of the emic-etic dichotomy. There are two kinds of typology, whose objects of classification are the same phenomena:

... 'first order constructs' or 'existential types': typifications or types constructed by participants in social systems. They are fundamental data for the social scientist and stand in contrast to, and yet in continuity with, the 'second order constructs' or 'constructed types' he develops and utilizes ... This suggests that there is a continuity between the typifying and concept-formation activity of action in social systems and that of social scientists ... (McKinney, 1969: 2).

Here the problem of concept-formation is once more presented in all its acuteness. All concepts are the result of a process of generalization, implying abstraction and reduction, and typification is an important aspect of this process:

... typification consists in the pragmatic reduction and equalization of attributes relevant to the particular purpose at hand for which the type has been formed and involves disregarding those individual differences of the typified objects that are not relevant to such purpose (*ibid.*: 3).

The result of this typification process as part of a whole methodological procedure is the typology, which ...

... must be understood as representative of a *pragmatic* research methodology and thus subject to evaluation in terms of the accuracy of predictions which result from its utilization (*ibid.*: 3).

In the latter quotation the emphasis is on the concept 'pragmatic'. The discussion as to whether typological configurations have an ontological existence in the realistic sense, or whether they are abstractions in a nominalistic sense, is secondary here. Of immediate importance for us is the intrinsic relation between typologizing and comparative study:

... the only kind of comparative generalization about cultural data that has been made and can be made is typological (Znaniecki, 1952: 179, in McKinney, 1969: 7).

The types which serve as starting-point for comparative generalizations may have different functions: they can be used for classificatory or descriptive ends; as heuristic devices and as methodological conveniences. We must make it explicit, however, that types function as theory, as was already said above:

... types represent phenomena in both a classificatory sense (a relation of similarity contrasting them with all other phenomena) and in systematic sense (structural-functional relations) ... (McKinney, 1969: 8-9).

The distinction between the properties of the *classificatory sense* and of the *systemic sense* is very important, because these properties can, I think, be used as taxonomic categories in designing typologies for classifying and systematizing e.g. a documentary stock of 'religious behaviour'.

Class	*System*
Relations of similarity	Relations of interconnectedness
Relations simple	Relations complex
Without form	Characteristic form
No quality of integration coordinated by similarity	Integrated-coordinated by interdependence
Members may be moved about without violence to them or to class	Units may not be moved about without violence to them or to system
No cohesion between members of a class	Functional consistency
An aggregate	A genuine whole, having a structure
The sum of its parts	Organic unity: not the sum of its constituent units

(Radcliff-Brown, 1957: 22, in McKinney, 1969: 9).

This survey of properties shows *int. al.* that

... the type is basically a *hypothetical or model* course of action, process, structure, system, object, etc. When using the type as an explanatory scheme, one is really saying, in a probabilistic sense, that this is the expected behavior of the sect ... or whatever the type may be (McKinney, 1969: 9).

Types and typologies are in any case useful as composite theoretical-methodological devices, though their operationalization and practical application to e.g. the iconography of science of religion still requires much preparatory work in the theoretical field.

As illustration, I give below a *minimum* list of basic categories of religious behaviour. The list is taken from Wallace and Yinger (co-determinant for typification were: the stress upon anthropological data, the incorporation of magic in the definition of religion and the restriction to supernatural systems).

1. Addressing the supernatural (prayer, exorcism);
2. Music (dancing, singing, chanting, playing instruments);
3. Physiological exercise (hysical manipulation of psychological states through drugs, deprivation, and mortification);
4. Exhortation (addressing others as representative of divinity);
5. Reciting the code (use of the sacred written and oral literature, which contains statements regarding the pantheon, cosmology, myths, and moral injunctions);
6. Simulation (imitating things for purposes of control);
7. *Mana* (touching things possessed of sacred power; laying on of hands);
8. *Taboo* (avoiding things to prevent the activation of unwanted power or undesired events);
9. Feasts (sacred meals);
10. Sacrifices (immolation, offerings, fees);
11. Congregation (processions, meetings, convocations);
12. Inspiration (pursuit of revelation, conversion, possession, mystical ecstasy);
13. Symbolism (manufacture and use of symbolic objects).

These are not tight analytic categories of religious behaviour, but they werve well to indicate the range. Perhaps they treat religion too much as a static and isolated system, and therefore we might extend them in two directions:

14. Extending and modifying the code (in connection with category 5);
15. Applying religious values in nonreligious contexts (... the consequential dimension).

(Yinger, 1970: 16, 17).

This list raises various questions, such as: on the grounds of what criteria can the 15 categories enumerated be called basic? If these are types of religious behaviour, and therefore 'phenomena in both a classificatory and a systemic sense' (see above), then what are the 'established criteria', i.e. the taxonomic criteria upon which such a list is based?

Obviously no fruitful operationalization is yet offered here of such theory formation now available as is relevant for the sciences of religion.

REFERENCES

Baal, J. van (1971), *Symbols for Communication. An Introduction to the Anthropological Study of Religion.* Assen, van Gorcum & Comp.
Baaren, Th. P. van (1973), 'Science of Religion as a Systematic Discipline,' in this volume, pp. 35ff.
La Barre, W. (1970), *The Ghost Dance. The Origins of Religion.* New York, Doubleday & Company.
Benedict, R. (1934), *Patterns of Culture.* New York, Houghton Mifflin.
Doorn, J. A. A. van and Lammers, C. J. (1967), *Moderne Sociologie. Systematiek en Analyse.* Utrecht/Antwerpen, Spectrum (Aula Boeken).
Driver, H. E. and Kroeber, A. L. (1932), 'Quantitative Expression of Cultural Relationships,' *University of California Publications in American Archaeology and Ethnology,* 31, pp. 211-256.
Drijvers, H. J. W. (1973), 'Theory Formation in Science of Religion and the Study of the History of Religions,' Chap. 3 in this volume.
Geertz, Clifford (1966), 'Religion as a Cultural System,' pp. 1-46 in Michael Banton (ed.), *Anthropological Approaches to the study of Religion.* London, Tavistock Publications.
Harris, M. (1968), *The Rise of Anthropological Theory; A History of Theories of Culture,* New York-London, Routledge & Kegan Paul.
Kluckhohn, C. (1953), 'Universal Categories of Culture,' pp. 507-523 in A. L. Kroeber (ed.), *Anthropology Today.* Chicago, University of Chicago Press.
Köbben, A. J. (1952), 'New Ways of Presenting an Old Idea: The Statistical Method in Social Anthropology,' *Journal of the Royal Anthropological Institute of Great Britain and Ireland,* 82 (1952), pp. 129-146.
Kroeber, A. L., and Kluckhohn, C. (1952), *Culture: A Critical Review of Concepts and Definitions.* Harvard University (Papers of the Peabody Museum of American Archaeology and Ethnology, vol. 47).
Leertouwer, L. (1973), 'Inquiry into Religious Behaviour,' Chap. 4 in this volume, pp. 79ff.
McKinney, J. C. (1969), 'Typification, Typologies, and Sociological Theory', *Social Forces,* 48, 1, pp. 1-12.

Moore, F. W. (ed.) (1961), *Readings in Cross-Cultural Methodology*. New Haven, Human Relations Area Files Press.

Murdock, G. P. (1940), 'The Cross-Cultural Survey,' *American Sociological Review*, 5, 3 (june 1940), pp. 361–370.

Murdock, G. P., a.o. (1967), *Outline of Cultural Materials*. New Haven, Human Relations Area Files Press.

Nadel, S. F. (1951), *The Foundations of Social Anthropology*. London, Cohen and West.

Pelto, P. J. (1970), *Anthropological Research. The Structure of Inquiry*. New York, Harper and Row.

Pike, K. (1954), *Language in Relation to a Unified Theory of the Structure of Human Behaviour*, vol. 1. Glendale, Calif., Summer Institute of Linguistics.

Radcliffe-Brown, A. R. (1957), *A Natural Science of Society*. Glencoe, Ill., The Free Press.

Spiro, M. E. (1951), 'Culture and Personality, The Natural History of a false Dichotomy,' *Psychiatry*, 14 (1951), pp. 19–46.

— (1966), 'Religion: Problems of Definition and Explanation,' pp. 85–126 in Michael Banton (ed.), *Anthropological Approaches to the Study of Religion*. London, Tavistock Publications.

Tennekes, J. (1971), *Anthropology, Relativism and Method*. Assen, van Gorkum & Comp.

Wallace, A. F. C. (1966), *Religion: An Anthropological View*. New York, Random House.

Yinger, J. M. (1970), *The Scientific Study of Religion*. London, Macmillan Company.

Znaniecki, F. (1952), *Cultural Sciences*. Urbana, Ill., University of Illinois Press.

Epilogue

The papers collected here, however diverse in content and tenor, have a common starting-point. In the preface, Van Baaren has already given an account of the method of work and the composition of the Groningen working-group which the authors have formed. The reader will have observed that the present volume is not the outcome of one particular 'school'. The various authors each go their own way, though often meeting in debate.

That which unites them can best be negatively described as a sense of insufficiency. They share the experience that the science of religion as taught and practised by them does not do justice to the subject of their study. Without wishing in any way to detract from the merits of their predecessors and contemporaries, they are of opinion that the systematic science of religion should follow other pathways than it has done thus far. This opinion of theirs is strengthened by association with their students who, less firmly rooted in the humanistic tradition than their teachers, can no longer be content with the mainly historical and literary approach to the phenomenon of religion alone. Their requirements in the field of systematic and comparative research can no longer be satisfied by the so-called phenomenology of religion.

It is not the place here to go into the causes of this situation. We will only quote the view of the Netherlands historian of religion, Dr. F. Sierksma, that 'science of religion, now as in the days of the *Aufklärung*, is a factor in the crisis of Christian civilization' (Sierksma, 1951). A fundamental change in the cultural position of religions such as we are experiencing, also makes other demands upon the scientific study of these religions. It is not for nothing that in these papers the question repeatedly appears how the researcher might get a grip upon processes of change within the religions. Entering into these and similar problems one finds that the methodical equipment of phenomenology of religion is in any case too restricted and has in many cases become useless.

The method which is the ideal of phenomenology of religion aims at a dialogue between one religious mind and another, resulting in a form of *Verstehen* which, if it does not preclude scientific explanation, certainly seriously impedes it. The social and cultural structures of the religions appear at best on the edges of the phenomenologist's field of vision; in how far they determine personal experience of religion or are, conversely, formed by it, remains obscure. As a result, science of religion as a systematic discipline does not sufficiently inspire the scientific study of religion in so far as this is carried out by disciplines based on socio-cultural structures. Conversely, it has not the means to adapt its *Wesensschau* in accordance with the work of sociologists, cultural anthropologists, social psychologists. The tension that existed from the beginning between phenomenology and historical science of religion, becomes isolation as soon as a single step is taken beyond the circle of historical and literary approaches. If, as it has been justly said, phenomenology is an art rather than a scientific method, then this entails that its adepts are faced with the task, amid the delicate apparatus of other sciences, of handling a complicated aggregate with the aid of a paintbrush or a sculptor's chisel.

That is the principal reason why the present volume has chosen a formula taken from cultural anthropology: religion is a function of culture. Besides the motives already mentioned, there is also a historical argument for this point of departure. From Söderblom until, and including, Van der Leeuw comparative religion derived both its methods of comparison and its theoretical concepts chiefly from the study of the religions of non-literate peoples, a sub-department of cultural anthropology. Even without taking over the evolutionism implicit in that procedure, it is apposite to begin a theoretical re-orientation in this sector. It is self-evident that this sector can be no more than a starting-point, as appears here, *inter alia*, in the paper of Drijvers.

The choice of the formula 'religion as a function of culture', though, is far from unambiguous and in itself admits of a plurality of methods. For a 'theory of religion' must offer an entry to all disciplines involved in this research, or still to be so involved; above all it may not *a priori* impose a hierarchy of methods, since the choice and sequence of the methods employed should depend upon the subject of research: a different choice is made for working on an Indian temple charter than for the study of ritual patterns in a Voodoo sect of Haiti.

So general an observation does not carry much weight. The various sub-disciplines of science of religion each have a selection of methods of their own; the advantages and disadvantages of each method usually appear in a quite different light when a method is related to others from a different sub-discipline. In this matter of making concepts from different disciplines operational with regard to a concrete subject of research, the papers collected here do not yet have much to contribute: they are more concerned with foundations than with methods. Of course matters cannot rest here; the true test is to seek a multi-disciplinary approach to a series of concrete problems and to provide an exact methodological account. At the same time, a better insight into these problems can be developed by making a methodological analysis of cases of already published research of a multi-disciplinary kind. There are some inceptions towards this in the present volume, especially where the various authors open a discussion with one another or with others as to the validity of methods and combinations of methods that they use.

In how far the formula 'religion is a function of culture' is a useful starting-point for different methodical approaches to religious phenomena also depends on the consistency of the hypotheses derived from the starting-point by the disciplines concerned. There is scope for a tremendous confusion of tongues around this point of departure. To counter this threat, science of religion will have to agree, *inter alia*, upon a platform of logical requirements to which statements must answer. These agreements are discussed by Hubbeling. His reasoning is an inducement to reopen a matter much neglected by the classical phenomenologists: the question whether experience of life and religious experience are admissible as sources of data for research. Hubbeling's view that classical logic is a sufficient touchstone for science of religion will seem reassuring to many of us who are not at home in the newer logical systems he deals with. Since however the kind of science of religion advanced in these papers expressly aims not only at *Verstehen* but also at explaining, there is a wide fallow field between Hubbeling's application of classical logic to science of religion and the other contributions, and further theoretical work will have to be done there to find the criteria to which explanations in science of religion will have to answer. For to explain means to reduce. The contribution of Van Baaren as well as the papers of Leertouwer and Waardenburg touch upon the question at what point an acceptable reduction passes into inadmissible reductionism; this point requires elucidation, since our discipline sprang from the nursery of theology, where reduction has always been kept within strict limits — too strict perhaps for a discipline which has no call to function as advocate for religion.

Let us return to the *content* of our common formula. We remarked above that this content was somewhat ambiguous. In Van Baaren's paper, where the formula is most fully worked out, the ambiguity is at least dispersed upon one point: he leaves no doubt that the view of religion as a function of culture means the exclusion of all philosophical or religious preconceptions. Not only is science of religion thus clearly distinguished from theology, but a provisional decision is also made as to the place and value in science of religion of statements made by the believers regarding their own religion. That impassioned yet necessary discussion in earlier phenomenology of religion about the religiosity of the researcher and about 'the faith of the believers' as the true hub of research — a discussion necessary because the phenomenological *Einfühlung* turned upon the communicating spark touched off between two forms of faith — can now be at an end. With Van Baaren the faith or unbelief of the researcher is at most of heuristic value, while 'the faith of the believers' as the real object of research is replaced by the relations of each religious phenomenon with other religious and non-religious phenomena within a particular culture.

We would here shortly touch upon some important consequences of this stand, if only because they play a material part in nearly every paper of the present collection. In the first place there is the sustained *cultural relativism* we see in Van Baaren's treatment of the theme. Discussion among cultural anthropologists since Benedict and Herskovits has shown that this attitude calls up a series of methodical problems, which could not be sufficiently gone into here (cf. Tennekes, 1971). For instance, if religion is to be derived from culture, this means that the individual's world of religious experience is made very largely subject of the cultural structure antecedent to the individual, which determines his experience.

In any case it is group expression which will be studied in the first place. The changed angle of vision demands a new approach to religious experience, a problem which has had no systematic attention in science of religion since William James and J. Wach.

A second consequence of our starting-point, closely connected with cultural relativism, is that a totally *different method of comparison* must be developed than that of phenomenology. Van Baaren gives us the essential criteria for this when he speaks of the 'principle of uncertainty', a religion being at the same time a unique phenomenon and also a component of a group of mutually comparable phenomena. It is a pressing task of further research, besides working out the 'principle of uncertainty', to test Van Baaren's model of religion as a structure built up of binary oppositions against related models in cultural anthropology and linguistics, the structuralism of Lévi-Strauss in particular.

A third point, also closely linked with the former two, is the dilemma of the *correct terminology*. We think Van Baaren is right to pay great attention to this. When it is no longer isolated phenomena, but rather patterns of relation between phenomena that are compared, high demands must be made both as to the formal character and the descriptive precision of the terms employed. Old style phenomenology suffered from imprecision in this matter, as even a superficial analysis of almost any index of a manual of science of religion will show. In Oosten's paper another terminological failing, also referred to by Van Baaren, is worked out in an instance concerned the conception of the soul: ethnocentrism in the naming and classification of religious phenomena.

The points we have named lead almost automatically to a fourth problem that is central in this volume and which, unlike the previous ones, has barely been treated explicitly by the authors. We mean the question what exactly we are to understand by culture in terms of science of religion. It is not possible to avoid this question by delegating it to a discipline such as cultural anthropology. First of all, because the matter is by no means agreed upon within that discipline, so that the choice of a particular definition always includes the choice of a particular approach to cultural functions, such as religion. More importantly, though, the hypotheses developed in this volume from the concept of culture evidence a strong preference for an abstract culture concept:

for Van Baaren and his group culture is a system, a scientific model rather than a piece of human reality. We can assume with Tennekes (1971: 78) that the opposition between abstraction and reality is an illusory paradox. The preference expressed in these papers certainly does not mean that we would lose sight of the empirical reality of culture: on the contrary indeed, for the farewell to traditional phenomenology also means turning towards a more empirical science. This implies, however, that the relation between the model and the reality both called 'culture' must be more thoroughly investigated than heretofore, and that an agreement must be arrived at as to the level of abstraction that is still acceptable without the link between reality and model being lost. This is of special importance for science of religion, which in research assigns a traditional primacy to religious conceptions rather than to values or behaviour — a primacy which Van Baaren thinks will continue to exist in a newer science of religion simply for practical reasons. Yet conceptions are rather abstract data. Hence the difficulties that crop up when we attempt to determine the mutual relation of conceptions and actual behaviour. For example, when Van Baaren distinguishes between symbolic and other religious behaviour, one can ask whether such a distinction can also hold good for conceptions. It is no simple matter to develop rules for this, especially when one reflects that the researcher must often take his knowledge of these conceptions from written texts, whose level of abstraction is already higher compared with actual religious ideas.

Leertouwer's paper therefore particularly aims at demonstrating how complicated the relation is between various kinds of conceptions, and between these and factual human behaviour in all its diversity. For human behaviour can be seen as the point of intersection between conceptions shaping and directing behaviour and the social reality in which the behaviour takes place and has its function. Regarded thus, the study of religious behaviour is pre-eminently suitable for a critical test of Van Baaren's description of religion; just what does the definition mean for the researcher's method of working, can he use it to connect up with other disciplines, in this case the behavioural sciences, and what model of relations then becomes apparent? Leertouwer's paper will have convinced the reader of the complicated difficulties attending the display of a model of relations: religious conceptions together with other conceptions determine human behaviour ('Religious belief is but one form of belief', Duncan), and it is very hard to determine exactly what part of behaviour can be marked down as religious. Discovering the frontiers of this *terra incognita*, however, is one of the gains of Van Baaren's description and Leertouwer's testing of it. The problems regarding 'religious experience' are analogous with this, as already remarked. Ultimately this problem can be reduced to the problem of the relation between ideas and social phenomena, which cannot be solved without the aid of the historical discipline, as Drijvers argues in his contribution. If one does not introduce the concept of change, ideas and social phenomena, religion and culture stand in a static relation to one another, in which it is easily attempted to explain religion by means of culture or culture by means of religion. Only by looking at human behaviour in a historical perspective — and all historical sources may be seen as 'congealed' human behaviour — can the factors be determined that rule the process of change, and which therefore dominate behaviour in a particular culture. It is only by working in this way that history of religions can be preserved from devoting all attention entirely to religious conceptions which are placed in a kind of timeless *Ideeëngeschichte*.

What difficulties remain to be mastered becomes clear when A.J. Vink's paper on taxonomy and classification of religious phenomena is laid beside the subject-indexes of the earlier handbooks of phenomenology, which are of an arbitrary nature when measured by the methodic demands of Vink. Much discussion will still be required on the subject whether renewed attention to religious behaviour is only the filling up of an historical lacuna, or whether it is the starting-point of an entirely new science of religion based on the methodic primacy of behaviour. Vink's choice is clearly the latter point of view. Further research must show whether such treatment of science of religion will not cause it to merge into a cultural anthropology based on cultural materialism. Should this prove to be the case, we shall have to consider what logical conclusions must then be drawn with regard to the identity of our discipline.

The historical approach advocated by Drijvers will also show us that the opposition between culture as an abstraction and as a reality is an illusory paradox. Modern socio-historical research is especially directed at solving this paradox by establishing many links between reality and the model. Also in the field of historical science of religion a closer scrutiny will thus reveal many possibilities of linking up with other disciplines, possibilities which are opened up and made necessary in Van Baaren's description of religion as a function of culture. Within the scope of the present work, the comparison of Leertouwer's and Drijvers's paper can be seen as a renewed plea for the collaboration of social and historical disciplines on the basis of a serviceable description that enforces a search for adequate methods.

Waardenburg follows another path when he wishes to leave classical phenomenology of religion behind him, in fixing his scientific attention upon 'meaning' of a religion in a culture. This meaning is not an objective datum as posited by earlier phenomenology of religion, but only exists as subjective meaning, meaning for the people concerned. Waardenburg studies religion as a form of human expression, so that only the relation between the religion and its adherents is relevant. It is true that the concrete situation and the general context of an individual or group must be taken into account, but these are only additional circumstances forming the background. The researcher must be able to put questions concerning the problems of human existence in order to gain access to the intentions of the religion and the meaning it supplies; to use Waardenburg's own words, he must be able 'to reconstruct the religious universe'. Obviously, having chosen this method, Waardenburg's preference is for living religions, where the adherents can directly answer the questions put to them. The relation between the student and the objects of his research is thus extremely close, both rationally and emotionally, so that Waardenburg can speak of the new style phenomenology of religion as a kind of cultural psychoanalysis. For this the researcher must himself go through an analysis bringing him a catharsis, after which he can view the subject of his study with fresh eyes and be capable of a real reconstruction. This form of phenomenology is therefore concerned with the meaning of religion, which is described as a signification system. Within this system, religion offers solutions for specific problems having to do with the 'ultimate sense of life', in other words: religion is a self-expression of human existence.

To be able to decide whether Waardenburg's attempt at conquering the problems of traditional phenomenology is successful, we can best

formulate a number of questions that arise after one has read his disquisition. Waardenburg posits that one must consult the accepted religion
in a culture to find out the meaning of life and reality for any given
bearer of this culture; for religion is concerned with the ultimate sense of
life. In how far has he, in this, left traditional phenomenology behind,
which regards every culture as a secularized cult, thus positing that it is
only in religion that the meaning of human existence is uncovered
(revealed)? When he speaks of subjective meaning, then in how far does
this concept differ from 'the faith of the believers', which the other authors
have in their papers declared to be the wrong angle of approach for
finding out the function of a religion? When to find the 'meaning' of a
religious phenomenon Waardenburg requires 'to reconstruct the religious
universe', then is that not really the same method as that to which Van
der Leeuw and others apply terms such as *Verstehen* and *Einfühlung*?
Can Waardenburg still explain religious phenomena if he reduces their
cultural context to such a distant background that the relation of the
'meaning' he finds to other belief- and value-systems does not show up at
all? Waardenburg refers to the isolation of Van der Leeuw and others
whose theological *parti pris* prevented their access to other problems than
those called up and also answered by that *parti pris* itself. Yet when he so
strongly accentuates subjective meaning and ultimate sense, then is that
not equally a *parti pris* that no longer admits of regarding religion as a
cultural variable? For Waardenburg's method contemporary religious
expressions are of fundamental importance, since only the researcher's
contemporaries can be questioned or studied in their religious behaviour.
Apart from the problems connected with putting questions as to the
meaning of something and working out the many very divergent answers — a matter in which the experience of the social sciences will prove
essential — one may well ask whether this is not a mere seeming advantage, that in the wide field of science of religion at once becomes a
disadvantage. For this method does not offer the possibility of profitable
historical comparisons, as it is extremely difficult to determine the
subjective meaning of certain phenomena for people who have long been
dead. Here we may refer to the attempts made in cultural anthropology
to overcome the disadvantages inherent in a study of phenomena in the
so-called anthropological present.

One might go on for some time in this way increasing the list of critical questions. The intention would not be to demonstrate the presumed weakness of Waardenburg's argumentation, but to examine all possibilities of renewal within traditional phenomenology where new ways are sought while preserving the values of the past. Waardenburg's paper demonstrates once again how strongly phenomenology is bound up with the crises of the Christian religion in Western culture. Between Van der Leeuw's view of religion as the human answer to a power revealing itself, and Waardenburg's view of religion as human self-expression answering questions after life and reality, there lies first of all a theological development of four decennia. Van Baaren inquires what cultural function of religion still subsists when a great number of persons in the culture concerned no longer feels any emotional or rational tie with that religion. This question is not dependent on theological developments, but on the loss of function of the Christian religion in Western culture. In such a situation it becomes urgent to find the function of religion *tout court*.

This epilogue has perhaps somewhat clarified positions and problematic, and pointed out possible ways of future research through the questions it raises. The discussion between the various authors will certainly be continued. If others will join in that discussion, the question after the function of religion will have proved its worth.

REFERENCES

Sierksma, F. (1951), *Freud, Jung en de religie.* Assen, Van Gorcum & Comp.
Tennekes, J. (1971), *Anthropology, Relativism and Method.* Assen, Van Gorcum & Comp.

Index of Names

Albert, H., 28
Aquinas, Thomas, 22-24
Argyle, M., 95
Aydelotte, W. O., 58, 64, 66

Baal, J. van, 94, 141
Baaren, Th. P. van, 42, 50, 52-53, 57-
    60, 64, 73, 79-81, 85-94, 96, 144,
    159, 162-166, 168
Baird, R. D., 57
Barre, W. La, 151
Becker, H., 143
Beek, W. E. A. van, 57
Benedict, R., 152, 162
Beth, E. W., 23-24, 29
Bianchi, U., 35, 48
Bleeker, C. J., 46, 58, 76
Bochenski, I. M., 29
Boskoff, A., 65-67
Bradbury, R. E., 53
Brain, R., 54
Braudel, F., 66
Brelich, A., 62, 80-81
Bunge, M., 29

Cahnman, W. J., 65-67, 69-70, 72
Cantwell Smith, W., 110
Carr, E. H., 66
Chantepie de la Saussaye, P. D., 45,
    116

Cochran, Th. C., 61
Codrington, R. H., 86
Cresswell, M. J., 30

Darwin, Ch. R., 61, 147
Dilthey, W., 49
Doorn, J. A. A. van, 141
Douglas, M., 74-75, 85
Driver, H. E., 148
Droysen, J. G., 28
Drijvers, H. J. W., 44, 85, 88, 160, 165-
    166
Dumont, L., 66
Duncan, H. D., 93, 165
Durkheim, E., 69-70, 144

Elias, N., 91, 103
Engels, F., 25, 146
Evans-Pritchard, E. E., 66-67

Finley, M. I., 61
Frazer, Sir J. G., 62
Freud, S., 28, 144
Frey, G., 16
Frick, H., 46, 51

Gadamer, H., 25
Geertz, C., 35-36, 64, 70, 86-87, 89,
    92, 99-101, 142, 144
Ginsberg, M., 148

Goldammer, K., 45, 52
Groot, A. D. de, 28, 99

Hardt, 37
Harris, M., 145-146, 148-149, 152
Harrison, J., 62
Hegel, G. W. F., 24-25, 115
Heidegger, M., 79
Heiler, F., 19
Helfer, J. S., 41, 43, 48, 50, 57
Helwig, P., 50
Hempel, C. G., 82
Herskovits, M. J., 162
Hobhouse, L. T., 143, 148
Hofstadter, R., 74
Horton, R., 91
Hubbeling, H. G., 30-31, 60-61
Hughes, G. E., 30
Husserl, E., 46

James, W., 163
Jensen, A. E., 72, 85
Jorgensen, J., 148

Kant, E., 115
Kiesel, Th., 28
Kippenberg, H. G., 59-60, 67
Kitagawa, J. M., 41
Kluckhohn, Cl., 70, 95, 141, 150
Köbben, A. J., 149
Kraemer, H., 50
Kraft, V., 29
Kristensen, W. B., 45, 73, 110, 116
Kroeber, A. L., 70, 95, 141, 148
Kuhn, Th. S., 28

Lammers, C. J., 141
Leertouwer, L., 59, 74-75, 138, 144, 162, 164-166

Leeuw, G. van der, 45, 48-50, 52, 79-80, 82-84, 86, 91, 115-116, 144, 160, 167-168
Lenin, W. I., 24-25
Leroi-Gourhan, A., 35
Lévi-Strauss, Cl., 37, 66, 100, 128, 163
Lewin, K., 51, 59, 82-83
Lewis, I. M., 43, 66, 71
Lipset, S. M., 66-68

MacGrew, R. E., 63, 66
MacKinney, J. C., 140, 153-154
Maes, J., 53
Malinowski, B., 36, 144, 148
Markov, 25
Marx, K., 25, 28, 146
Mensching, G., 63
Metzger, W. P., 61, 71
Miller, R. J., 80
Moore, F., 150
Morgenstern, C., 81
Morton, M. I., 95
Murdock, G. P., 140, 142, 148-149

Nadel, S. F., 89, 95, 138-139, 142-143
Norbeck, E., 35

Obbink, H. W., 43
Oosten, J. G., 163
Opp, K. D., 82
Otto, R., 40, 45

Pannenberg, W., 31
Pelto, P. J., 144-145
Piddington, R., 36
Pike, K., 149
Plessner, H., 75, 86
Pollock, A., 54
Preuss, H. Th., 86

Radcliffe-Brown, A.R., 143, 154
Radin, P., 85
Robertson Smith, W., 62
Rudolph, K., 61, 94

Schiller, F., 61
Schilling, W., 49
Schiwy, G., 37
Schleiermacher, F.D.E., 94
Schneider, B., 39
Schneider, D.M., 87
Sierksma, F., 49, 52, 159
Slicher van Bath, B.H., 72
Smith, M., 44, 58-59
Söderblom, N., 160
Sorokin, P., 63, 70
Spencer, H., 148
Spiro, M.E., 36, 64, 71-72, 86, 87-89, 92, 101, 138, 141, 143, 151
Stalin, J., 25
Stegmüller, W., 28
Steinmetz, S.R., 148
Suttles, W., 151
Swanson, G.E., 36

Tennekens, J., 89, 95, 139, 141, 162, 164
Theophrastus, 30

Toynbee, A.J., 63
Turner, V.W., 37, 82-83
Tylor, E.B., 148

Vayda, A., 151
Vetter, G.B., 42
Vink, A.J., 165
Voget, F.W., 74
Vogt, E.Z., 67, 69, 70, 73

Waardenburg, J.D.J., 162, 166-168
Wach, J., 45, 163
Wagenvoort, H., 84
Wallace, A.F.C., 155
Wartofsky, M.W., 28
Weber, M., 63-64, 67-70, 144
Wheeler, G.C., 148
Widengren, G., 76, 80, 144
Wiese, L. von, 143
Winch, P., 103
Worsley, P., 89

Yinger, J.M., 101, 152, 155

Zaehner, P.C., 43
Znaniecki, F., 154
Zorn, 24